LEAN SHOP
MAKEOVER

LEAN SHOP
MAKEOVER

LEARN HOW TO DRIVE OUT WASTE AND SUBSTANTIALLY IMPROVE LEAD TIME AND PROFITABILITY

JOHN S. HACKLEY | ASBC

CERTIFIED

(H)

WRITTEN
BY HUMAN

ACKNOWLEDGMENTS

I want to express my gratitude to everyone who supported me in writing this book.

I am incredibly thankful to my editor, Jeff Wooten, whose patience and keen insights have greatly improved the quality of this book. His expertise and guidance were invaluable, helping me refine my thoughts and present them clearly.

Finally, I want to express my deepest gratitude to all my extraordinary mentors, dedicated coaches, talented employees, and valued clients, both those who have been part of my journey in the past and those who are currently by my side. Your unwavering support, insightful guidance, and encouragement have played a crucial role in shaping my path and helping me grow.

Thank you all for being an integral part of this adventure; I couldn't have done it without you!

CONTENTS

Acknowledgments...5
Preface 9
Foreword 11
Testimonials...13
Introduction 17

1. Four Stages of Team Building 31
2. Recruiting the Right Players 37
3. Hire Slow, Fire Fast!...45
4. Developing Your Team..49
5. Position Agreements 55
6. Functional Cross-Training 63
7. Lean Production Philosophy..73
8. Lean Into Quality With QCD 83
9. Lean 5S Gets More Work Done Faster 91
10. Benefits of Improving OEE 99
11. Concepts of Kaizen 109
12. Lean Shop Management System...121

Frequently Asked Questions...129
What Clients Can Expect From Us..135
What Do You Get When Working With Us? 137
Transformation Is a Four-Step Process.....................................139
Lean Shop Makeover Programs 143
Putting It All Together..145
About Our Team 147

PREFACE

You are sitting on a gold mine and don't even know it!!

It's truly remarkable how life can unfold. I'm writing to you now as a published author, which I never would have imagined for myself, but it feels fitting, and I can embrace it fully.

What stands out to me is that the journey to writing this book has been significant. It took a lifetime of accumulated knowledge and expertise, along with two years of writing and refining the manuscript following the onset of the COVID-19 pandemic in 2020.

During this time, my consulting business paused, giving me the opportunity for some soul-searching. I realized that I needed to differentiate myself as a consultant—finding a clearer way to articulate my message and approach. Thus, a transformation began, focusing on rebranding and specializing in Lean manufacturing principles.

The essence of *Lean Shop Makeover*, which you are about to read, serves as a foundational starting point for unlocking the wealth within your organization—wealth you may not even know exists. This was my experience when I committed to transforming my business by implementing lean principles, the same which I'll share with you today.

So, if you own and operate a signage or custom job shop and are not achieving the success you envisioned as a leader, take a moment to reflect. You have a remarkable opportunity waiting to be discovered within your shop—a treasure trove of potential revenue hidden just beneath the surface.

My mission is to guide you in uncovering the strategies and techniques that will empower your business to thrive, revealing the wealth within your craft. Together, we can elevate your current efforts and transform them into a thriving venture that generates the profits and freedom you've always dreamed of. The journey starts here!

FOREWORD

"If anyone can make you a disciple of Lean manufacturing, it's John and the Lean Shop Manager team."
— Jeff Wooten, 25-year editor of *Sign Builder Illustrated*

I have known John professionally for nearly fifteen years (give or take a year or two or three), ever since he reached out to me and solicited his first article idea while I was editing one of the premier how-to trade magazines of the sign industry. After reading John's initial pitch about shop organization, I really didn't know what to expect.

Most of the articles we were publishing at the time, written either first-hand from shop owners or pieced together through interviews with them, focused mainly on the nuts and bolts of how projects were fabricated and installed. There really weren't any stories with anyone asking, "Well, how are we going to de-clutter and organize our shop floor, get everyone on the same page, and be able to complete our customer's request on time and within budget?"

To me, the manufacturing world has always placed more emphasis toward the ingredients, the operating skills, and the physical know-how when creating projects for clients. But there's a lot more (a...lot... more!) to the process that can easily get overlooked—if even asked at all—by manufacturing companies owners. I am talking about things like the sales process, ergonomics, scheduling, workflow, employee management, etc.

John's first written piece for us (and response to it) eventually turned into a large series of articles that expanded into discussions about concepts like 5S, workflow logjam solutions, and, yes, Lean manufacturing. These were eye openers! This was information our audience also needed to know about and be able to implement.

I am pretty certain that, at the time, many manufacturing professionals probably thought more about healthy eating when the word "Lean" was mentioned in any production philosophy that had come across up until that point. In my opinion, John's business- and management-oriented articles ended up being just as valuable when it came to our readers' shop success as much as showing how one shop built this or another shop created that.

And as you'll see while reading *Lean Shop Makeover*, John possesses the ability to confidently explain concepts like muda and Kaizen that could be foreign to you. He will address topics like strategically building your team, functional cross-training, Lean production philosophy, and finally the benefits of his Lean Shop Management System™. The even-better news is that all the pointers he makes for signage can really be adapted to any manufacturing industry.

So, repeating my initial statement, if anyone can make a shop or production manager a Lean manufacturing convert, it's John. Enjoy this publication!

Jeff Wooten is the former editor of Sign Builder Illustrated *magazine, as well as a writer and editor with twenty-five years of experience covering topics such as signage, digital displays, safety/OSHA, installation, marketing, and more. He has also hosted podcasts and webinars related to a variety of sign industry-related subjects.*

TESTIMONIALS

Testimonial 1: "If you are thinking of hiring John to help you increase your shop's throughput and quality, then you are about to work with one of the most knowledgeable, professional, process-oriented, and personable consultants in the industry. John knows what he is doing, and if you follow his lead and go through his different processes then you will see a dramatic and positive difference in your business."

—M. Pertsis, General Manager

Testimonial 2: "I met John a few years ago when we worked on a project together. We have continued to collaborate on many levels within the industry. He is a consummate professional who really knows what he's talking about....and he backs it up with action that gets results. Whether it's business development, manufacturing, or sales, I know I can trust him for practical solutions and he's always available with an upbeat attitude. If your business is struggling and needs help, I highly recommend you call John. You'll be glad you did."

—P. Quattrocchi, General Manager

Testimonial 3: "Hey John, thank you so much! I am so enjoying the program! Totally finding it inspirational!"

—J. Collins, Owner

Testimonial 4: "We have seen inventory turns increase in less than 12 months, which contributes significantly to the cash collection process & bottom line. Another critical outcome is the enhanced connectivity across departments, which has regained internal trust and reliability, which makes everyone more effective. Culture is now more open to collaborate, challenge, and change for the greater good of customers & the enterprise."

—M. McKeag, President

Testimonial 5: "I joined the company after they had begun working with Oculus Business Solutions. While some team members were resistant to change, everyone who stayed with the program eventually saw that we benefited from the weekly teaching modules we were introduced to, which benefited us daily from project to project.

I can only assume that before we learned Oculus's project value chain process, completing any job for any client must have been frustratingly tricky because there was no standard process. Chaos ruled supreme.

Working with John requires a beginner's mindset and to quit assuming you have all the answers. Once you are open to his tutelage, John has excellent insight into making every business function make sense and communicating those values to everyone on your team.

Internally, as a team, we have gained personal accountability. We have a process flow where each team member has a role in enacting change. Externally, we can demand a higher price point because our clients can expect flawless execution when we follow the Oculus process.

In the short time I have been working with John, I have seen my thought process change for the better...In my professional and personal life."

—N. Jones, Client Services Manager

Testimonial 6: "John came on our radar late last year. After several months of exploratory conversations and due diligence, we hired John as a business coach and growth strategist.

In a short time, John's process has transformed the way we think, introduced us to improved systems, KPI reporting, and many other things that are real game changers for us. We've grown more in three months than we have over the past three years!

John owns and commands all that he preaches and has delivered more than expected. In an ever-changing business climate, John has become a foundation of strength and knowledge to build upon as Husky Creative looks forward to a bright future."

—M. Johnson, Owner

Testimonial 7: "Our production staff has really grasped the Oculus management system. Our on-time percentage has steadily increased with the biggest win so far, which came last week, where we're now up to 85% on reorders…before was hit and miss at best. That is the highest it has been in a LONG time!"

—R. Hudnut, Senior Project Manager

Testimonial 8: "What John counts most is the intangible part he plays in people's lives. He has made it possible for hundreds of people to support their families including, through his influence, me and my own. Dreaming and making are like breathing in and breathing out for John.

—R. Chambers, Ph.D., CEO

Testimonial 9: "John's Value Chain System is far and away the best in the industry. Materials flow seamlessly in one end of the shop and out the other as a finished product without rework or callbacks. Along the way, every machine and worker has a specific task responsibility, which is sequenced to complete projects on time and always with exceptional quality."

—B. Wilcox, Production Manager

Testimonial 10: "Through John's 'Fresh Eyes,' he helped us see the company from a new perspective, which kick-started a much-needed improvement initiative. His systems, insights, and experience led us to change the way we were doing business —from identifying core issues that needed to be addressed to highlighting employee interests and concerns to shore up morale.

Additionally, he provided great solutions from re-balancing staff responsibilities for more streamlined communication and improved teamwork to providing suggestions for new plant configurations to maximize workflow, making our fabrication processes easier and more productive."

—Jeff Osicka, General Manager

Testimonial 11: "Thanks to John and Oculus Business Coaching, we are now operating with results never realized before. Work is being completed many times faster with less uncertainty and rework. I highly recommend John to any shop wanting to raise their production game and make more money with less stress."

—S. Valdez, Operations Manager

INTRODUCTION

The Lean Shop Management System™ (LSMS) is a streamlined framework that integrates the proven principles of the Theory of Constraints (TOC) with Lean flow manufacturing methodologies. This introduction provides a comprehensive understanding of the benefits of implementing LSMS in your organization.

In modern business, companies universally strive to achieve several key objectives: securing a competitive advantage, maximizing profitability, and expanding their market share. In pursuit of these goals, organizations must recognize that contemporary customers have heightened expectations. They demand high-quality products that meet their specifications and are delivered punctually. Furthermore, today's consumers are increasingly prone to shift their loyalty; they are willing to explore alternative suppliers who can satisfy their criteria for quality, timely delivery, and cost-effectiveness.

The challenges are further compounded by the reality of the global economy, where competition can arise from any corner of the world and frequently from countries with lower labor costs. This dynamic creates an urgent need for companies to differentiate themselves in the marketplace.

However, visionary managers refuse to be disheartened by these obstacles. Instead, they see the opportunity to adapt and evolve as a crucial aspect of maintaining and enhancing their competitive position.

They recognize that the ability to consistently meet or exceed customer expectations provides a significant edge over rivals. Consequently, a growing number of organizations are adopting Lean manufacturing principles as a strategic approach to not only achieve operational efficiency but also to foster continuous improvement. By doing so, they aim to enhance their overall performance, cultivate customer loyalty, and solidify their presence in an increasingly competitive market.

Today, Lean practitioners across various industries are reported to experience significant and sometimes extraordinary financial and performance benefits due to the implementation of Lean manufacturing principles. Every day, innovative managers and leaders recognize that the tools and techniques associated with Lean manufacturing are not only powerful but also remarkably straightforward to apply. The advantages gained by organizations that have embraced Lean methodologies typically include the following:

Inventory Reduction: One of the most compelling outcomes of adopting Lean practices is a dramatic reduction in work-in-process inventory. It's not uncommon for companies to achieve reductions of 90% or more. This decrease not only minimizes the amount of capital tied up in inventory but also streamlines the production process, allowing for a more efficient flow of materials.

Quality Improvements: Implementing Lean practices necessitates rigorous documentation and standardization of processes. By focusing on creating error-proof procedures and enforcing quality standards at each step of production, companies often see a significant decline in scrap rates and the need for rework. This improvement in quality not only enhances customer satisfaction but also reduces costs associated with defects.

Enhanced Productivity: Training employees to perform standardized work with an emphasis on maintaining high-quality standards can result in substantial productivity gains. Even organizations that are considered mature or established in their industries have witnessed impressive increases in output and efficiency, allowing them to optimize resource utilization and meet production demands more effectively.

Improved Response Time to Customer Orders: In today's fast-paced market landscape, the ability to quickly respond to customer needs has shifted from being a competitive advantage to a necessity. By eliminating waste, especially in queue times, Lean manufacturing systems allow companies to manufacture products significantly faster than traditional methods. This agility enables businesses to adapt to market changes and customer preferences swiftly, ultimately enhancing customer loyalty.

Reduction in Working Capital Requirements: Effective management of working capital is crucial for the sustainability of any business. Lean manufacturing principles can substantially reduce the necessity for working capital by optimizing inventory levels and improving cash flow. In some cases, businesses have been able to eliminate their reliance on external financing, thereby reducing financial risk and enhancing operational stability.

Improved Floor Space and Capital Asset Utilization: By reorganizing and linking manufacturing processes into cohesive flow lines or cells, companies can achieve a marked improvement in floor space utilization. The related reduction in work-in-progress (WIP) inventory, coupled with a commitment to maintaining a clean and organized production environment, can result in a 20% or greater reduction in the amount of factory floor space necessary for operations. This means that organizations can optimize their existing space and potentially defer expensive expansion costs.

While implementing Lean manufacturing practices does not come with a guaranteed success formula, the methodologies have been successfully employed by thousands of companies worldwide, yielding tangible results. To embark on this transformative journey, it is essential for organizations to cultivate a companywide commitment to Lean principles, starting with enthusiastic support and engagement from top management. This commitment sets the foundation for fostering a culture of continuous improvement and operational excellence within the organization.

DETAILED ANALYSIS OF CALCULATING BENEFITS

The benefits of Lean manufacturing are often discussed in broad terms, but company management requires specific, quantifiable evidence of these advantages to justify implementation. They seek assurance that Lean manufacturing initiatives will translate into measurable financial improvements that positively affect the company's bottom line. When management has confidence that a Lean project will yield significant dollar savings in a relatively short timeframe, the approval process tends to be expedited. Conversely, if the anticipated benefits are perceived as minimal, complex, risky, or likely to manifest only after a long delay, the proposed Lean manufacturing project may encounter considerable resistance during the approval stage.

Fortunately, the potential financial gains from transitioning to a Lean manufacturing model can be substantial, especially for organizations shifting away from traditional, functional manufacturing techniques. For example, companies that effectively implement Lean practices could experience a remarkable reduction in WIP inventory, potentially by up to 90%. This significant decrease can lead to improved cash flow and reduced storage costs. Additionally, a similar 90% reduction in factory response time can be achieved, resulting in faster production cycles, enhanced customer satisfaction, and a stronger competitive edge in the market.

To facilitate the approval process, it is essential to clearly articulate these potential benefits. Justifying Lean implementation does not need to be an overwhelming task; the financial metrics alone can provide a compelling case. The anticipated reductions in both finished goods and WIP inventory can serve as powerful selling points for the program.

CURRENT	BENEFIT	MEASURE	PROPOSED
10,000	Floor Space Used	Total Square Feet	6,000
412	Total Part Travel	Linear Feet	220
2	Number of Operators Required	Head Count	2
0	Number of Support Personnel	Head Count	2
$15,040	Work in Process Inventory	Dollars	$2,500
20	Unit per Labor Hour	Units	40
$56.00	Cost per Piece	Dollars	$32.00
12	Manufacturing Lead Time	Days	4
3	Housekeeping Rating	5S Weighting	4
65%	Value Added Ratio	Percentage	85%

Highlighting these significant improvements in efficiency and cost-effectiveness will not only foster a better understanding of the Lean initiative but will also increase the likelihood of swift approval from management. Overall, a comprehensive presentation of the detailed benefits associated with Lean manufacturing is crucial for overcoming the obstacles to its implementation.

Enhancing operational efficiency is a complex challenge that often requires more than just superficial changes. Many organizations have been actively pursuing improvement initiatives for extended periods, and as a result, they may have already captured many of the easily attainable benefits. However, deeper exploration may uncover further opportunities for improvement and cost savings. It is important to understand that the process of enhancing operations is an ongoing journey rather than a finite project. There are seven detailed areas to investigate when estimating the potential benefits of implementing Lean manufacturing principles:

Work-in-Process (WIP) Inventory: WIP inventory plays a critical role in determining the speed and efficiency of production flows within the factory. For example, if a company's average response time can be reduced from five days to one day, the associated WIP inventory should ideally decrease by about 80%. This significant reduction can lead to faster turnaround times, improved customer satisfaction, and lower holding costs.

Finished Goods Inventory (FGI): When factory response times are optimized, it directly impacts the amount of finished goods necessary to maintain target service levels for customers. Companies should approach reductions in FGI cautiously—initially maintaining slightly higher inventories until the desired line performance is consistently demonstrated. Once reliable data confirms improved throughput, more significant cuts to FGI can be safely applied.

Raw Materials Management: A common misconception among companies is that raw material reductions should be prioritized above all else. However, it is often more beneficial to exclude raw material savings from preliminary analyses, as they are more aligned with supply-chain management than with line response time. Implementing tools like supplier Kanban systems can effectively manage and balance raw material levels, ensuring that supplies are available when needed while reducing excess inventory.

Standard Work and Waste Reduction: Streamlining processes through standardization, eliminating non-value-added activities, and reducing waste can lead to remarkable improvements in productivity, typically in the range of 15-20%. Although quantifying these enhancements can be challenging in the initial phases, it is crucial to approach any claims about productivity gains with caution, emphasizing the need for ongoing evaluation and refinement of processes.

Scrap and Rework Analysis: Understanding the costs associated with scrap and rework is vital, as these elements often contribute unseen expenses that distort productivity measurements. Identifying the root causes of high scrap rates can lead to targeted solutions. If these issues stem from workmanship deficiencies, organizations can expect substantial improvements by deploying well-structured standard work, utilizing check-do-check techniques, and establishing comprehensive training and certification programs. However, if scrap issues are linked to more complex factors such as machine processes or design flaws, these will require a more extended focus to resolve, though resolution remains crucial for long-term efficiency.

Overtime Management: Lean manufacturing tools are invaluable when it comes to controlling and reducing overtime costs, which can erode profit margins. A production line should be designed with a target volume that typically surpasses current demand levels. By accurately matching labor resources to production needs, businesses can significantly minimize the occurrence of unplanned overtime and its associated expenses.

Overhead Cost Reduction: Overhead costs often account for 15-25% of overall product costs, and because many of these expenses are non-value-added, there exists a substantial opportunity for cost reduction. Identifying specific areas where overhead can be trimmed—such as administrative inefficiencies, excessive utility expenses, and redundant processes—can lead to significant operational savings.

By thoroughly examining these critical areas, organizations can uncover hidden potentials for improvement and realize the full benefits of Lean manufacturing practices. Emphasizing a continuous improvement mindset will help ensure that these enhancements are sustainable, creating long-term value for the business and its stakeholders.

Lean manufacturing is an efficient and economical approach to operational improvement that focuses on minimizing waste while maximizing productivity. The main costs associated with this strategy include comprehensive training for employees and the time needed to implement essential changes within the organization. Fortunately, the required capital investment is typically low compared to other initiatives aimed at improving operational efficiency.

One of the most compelling aspects of Lean manufacturing is its potential for significant returns on investment. Even when using conservative estimates, companies can expect a payback ratio of anywhere from 5:1 to 10:1, or even greater over time. This impressive return on investment highlights the effectiveness of Lean practices in enhancing operational efficiency, reducing costs, and increasing overall profitability.

Moreover, implementing Lean manufacturing practices can be one of the best investments a company can make. By streamlining processes, reducing waste, and improving product quality, organizations not only enhance their competitiveness in the market but also create a culture of continuous improvement. Compared to other investment opportunities, few provide the same level of financial return or improvement in productivity that Lean manufacturing offers.

PROPOSING A PROVEN SET OF TOOLS

When advocating for the implementation of Lean manufacturing practices within your organization, it is crucial to present a well-established and low-risk methodology that stakeholders can trust. One effective option is the **Lean Shop Management System™ (LSMS)**. This system is not only proven but also incorporates various Lean manufacturing tools that have been designed to be straightforward, consistent, and repeatable throughout diverse applications.

The Lean manufacturing tools associated with the **LSMS** offer significant advantages, primarily by providing a framework for standardizing business processes. This standardization helps to create a streamlined flow of operations, which is essential for enhancing efficiency and reducing waste. Over the years, these tools have demonstrated their effectiveness in a wide range of environments, tackling various challenges such as different types of products, product mixes, levels of customization, and production volumes. They have been successfully employed in both machine-intensive and labor-intensive settings, making them versatile across industries and cultural contexts.

These tools are crafted to not only support your intuition but also to augment your expertise regarding your products and internal processes. By utilizing these methodologies, you can leverage both your knowledge and the structured approach provided by the **LSMS** for improved outcomes.

As you explore the path laid out by the **LSMS**, it's vital to meticulously document each step of your journey. This documentation not only helps in keeping track of your progress but also serves as a reference for future implementations. By doing so, you significantly enhance your chances of achieving successful outcomes and fostering a culture of continuous improvement within your organization.

Always keep in mind that while these tools are incredibly valuable, the ultimate responsibility for designing the production line rests with you and your team. The purpose of these tools is to assist and facilitate your efforts, not to replace your insight and creativity. By combining your expertise with the proven methodologies of the **LSMS**, you can drive significant improvements in your operational processes.

FINDING A TOP-MANAGEMENT OWNER

Identifying a committed top-management owner is crucial for achieving success in any initiative, but it is especially vital when it comes to implementing Lean manufacturing practices. Lean manufacturing involves a comprehensive system of tools and techniques designed to enhance efficiency and quality while minimizing waste. Despite the apparent simplicity of these tools, the scale of transformation required to fully integrate Lean principles into an organization can be extensive and complex.

As organizations shift towards Lean manufacturing, several fundamental changes occur within the company. First, employee roles may be redefined, leading to new responsibilities and expectations. Performance metrics, traditionally used to evaluate success, may also need to be revised to align with Lean objectives. Furthermore, the way work is conducted will change; processes may be streamlined, and collaboration may be emphasized more than before. Additionally, the physical workspace might undergo modifications to promote efficiency and foster a culture of continuous improvement.

What was once deemed acceptable behavior in the workplace—actions that were synonymous with being a diligent and compliant employee— can suddenly become counterproductive and hinder the company's ability to compete effectively in the market. This shift highlights the necessity for a cultural and operational transformation that can only be successful if it is supported by engaged leadership.

A top-management owner is essential to drive this transformation. Their involvement not only provides the necessary authority to implement changes but also sets the tone for the entire organization. The ideal approach is one that is unwavering and comprehensive, with the top management team fully aware of the potential benefits of Lean manufacturing. They should collectively champion the initiative, motivating and enabling a dedicated team to carry out the transition effectively.

In summary, successful implementation of Lean manufacturing requires not just a change in tools and processes but also a significant shift in the organization's culture and leadership approach. A committed top-management owner can ensure that this transformation is embraced at all levels of the organization, ultimately leading to improved competitiveness and success.

UNCOVERING A LEAN CHAMPION

In every successful Lean implementation project, one of the most critical components is identifying and nurturing a strong Lean champion within the organization. This individual is the most dedicated advocate for Lean principles, possessing a deep belief in the potential benefits of Lean methodologies. Their position or rank within the company is irrelevant; they may come from any level of the organization, and their background may vary widely in terms of gender, education, and experience.

The Lean champion plays a vital role in grasping the core concepts of Lean manufacturing. They invest time and effort into comprehending how these principles apply specifically to the company's unique processes, challenges, and opportunities for improvement. Their ability to visualize the results of Lean initiatives not only motivates them but also inspires others in the organization to embrace the Lean journey.

In addition to being passionate, the Lean champion actively participates in all phases of the Lean project—from the initial planning stages to the final execution of Lean practices. Their involvement is crucial in ensuring that the team remains aligned with the goals of the implementation, and they often serve as a liaison between different departments, facilitating communication and collaboration.

To successfully find a Lean champion, it is essential to look beyond traditional boundaries and departmental silos. This person may come from manufacturing, administration, finance, or even customer service; the key factor is their enthusiasm for continuous improvement and problem-solving. By recognizing that Lean practices can benefit the entire organization, you avoid the common pitfall of limiting Lean efforts to only the operational side of the business, which can result in missed opportunities for overall enhancement.

Investing in the development of this Lean champion is crucial. Providing opportunities for education, mentoring, and practical experiences will enable them to grow in their understanding and capabilities. This support not only empowers the Lean champion to excel in their role but also fosters a culture of learning and improvement throughout the organization, ultimately leading to enhanced performance and results.

RELYING ON PEOPLE FROM THE START

At the core of successful Lean manufacturing lies the invaluable contribution of the people who operate and manage the processes. These individuals are not just workers; they are integral team members whose insights and experiences are crucial for optimizing efficiency and productivity. Lean manufacturing hinges on the philosophy that every employee can offer unique perspectives to improve operations, and their active involvement is essential for continuous improvement.

The traditional viewpoint that regards shop floor employees merely as hands and feet—utilitarian resources with little input—can severely limit the potential for success. This narrow perspective fosters an environment where employees feel undervalued and disengaged, leading to diminished motivation and creativity. As a result, even if the shop floor appears to embody the principles of Lean manufacturing, without the full engagement of its workforce, it is destined to underperform and struggle with inefficiency.

In contrast, when employees are encouraged to participate in discussions about process improvements, share their ideas, and take ownership of their roles, the shop floor transforms into a collaborative space. This participatory approach not only boosts morale but also empowers employees to take initiative in problem-solving and innovation. Consequently, this leads to a dynamic of continual enhancement where processes are optimized, waste is minimized, and overall performance is significantly improved. Without this foundational involvement of the workforce, the dream of a Lean manufacturing environment will remain unfulfilled, functioning instead as a stagnant or ineffective system.

IT'S NOT A SOFTWARE PROJECT

We want to clarify right from the beginning that our stance is not against the use of software. In fact, we hold a strong belief in the value of software tools in enhancing the processes of documenting, calculating, and storing vital information related to the design and implementation of Lean processes. These tools can significantly streamline workflows and improve accuracy in data management. However, it's crucial to understand that software should not be seen as a substitute for essential human attributes such as common sense, discipline, and a comprehensive understanding of the products and processes that you intend to integrate into a Lean environment.

Our experience has shown that many Lean implementation projects can falter or even come to a complete halt when they are overly reliant on software rather than being directed by knowledgeable and empowered individuals. Software systems may possess advanced functionalities, but they lack the critical thinking capabilities necessary for decision-making, particularly in the context of Lean manufacturing. This decision-making requires not only technical knowledge but also an understanding of the unique nuances of the specific manufacturing environment and the people involved.

Moreover, discipline is a fundamental element of successful Lean implementations, and that cannot be instilled by software alone. The choice of software products should be a thoughtful one, ensuring that they align seamlessly with the principles of the Lean environment. Instead of adjusting the Lean methodologies to fit the capabilities or deficiencies of the software systems, it is imperative that the tools enhance and support the Lean philosophy.

Based on our extensive experience designing and implementing Lean manufacturing systems in a variety of organizations across different industries, we would like to emphasize a few key points: Lean manufacturing is not an enigmatic or mystical process; it is a practical approach grounded in fundamental principles. While it may seem challenging at times, it is far from impossible, and it is not exclusively reserved for a select group of practitioners. In fact, engaging in Lean manufacturing can be a rewarding and enjoyable journey that brings teams together and fosters a culture of continuous improvement.

CHAPTER 1

Four Stages of Team Building

"Coming together is a beginning. Keeping together is progress. Working together is a success."

— Henry Ford

Achieving success, whether in business, sports, or any other endeavor, is a gradual process that entails consistent effort, perseverance, and resilience. Success rarely happens overnight and is often accompanied by various challenges and setbacks that test one's determination. This has held true not only in the 1900s but also remains relevant today.

Regardless of the era, the evolution of team building has been a constant aspect in achieving success. In 1965, Bruce Tuckman introduced a model that outlines the four distinct stages necessary for a team to develop and grow. These stages include forming, storming, norming, and performing—highlighting the essential phases that teams go through in their journey toward effectiveness and high performance. Tuckman's model provides valuable insights into the dynamics of team development and offers a framework for understanding and managing the challenges that teams face as they strive for success. Let's take a closer look at his team-building model now:

STAGE 1 | FORMING

During the forming stage, team members engage in the process of mutual understanding and relationship building. They seek to identify individual strengths, weaknesses, and quirks to clearly understand how each member can contribute to the group. Additionally, they aim to gauge when each member can be relied upon and learn about potential concerns or conflicts. This stage also involves a focus on understanding the overall objectives and goals of the team, as well as the practical details of the tasks at hand, including who will be involved, what needs to be done, when it needs to be completed, and where the work will take place.

Furthermore, team members tend to work independently during this stage while simultaneously gaining insight into their own roles—as well as the roles of their fellow team members—within the broader team structure.

At this stage, the leader's role is critical in guiding the team to establish clear objectives and delineate team roles and responsibilities. The leader may need to adopt a more directive approach to provide clear guidance for the team or group.

However, it's important to note that this phase can be frustrating for many individuals due to the extensive focus on information gathering, which is time-consuming. As a result, actions are often put on hold until a clear direction is determined.

STAGE 2 | STORMING

As individuals become more secure within the team, they may start to challenge the established boundaries of the forming stage, potentially leading to the emergence of conflicts. These clashes are often rooted in differing personalities and varied working styles, which can have a detrimental impact on the team's overall performance as previously hidden resentments and irritations come to the surface. In response, the team needs to collectively address these issues, devising strategies to overcome the inevitable challenges and misunderstandings that arise as the project progresses.

While competition may still exist, individuals also start to open up to one another. Through this growing openness, the team starts to define and solidify the ways in which it will collaborate and work together moving forward.

During this phase, the leader should be highly accessible, so as to ensure effective communication and support for team members. It is common for team members to challenge the leader's decisions or vie for prominent team positions. The leader must clearly communicate the responsibilities and tasks assigned to each team member, in order to maintain team cohesion and progress. Providing individual coaching and support may be necessary to address challenges with team members who display resistance or struggle to fulfill their tasks. At times, the leader may need to assume a more directive role, so as to uphold professionalism within the team and facilitate the resolution of conflicts in an impartial manner conducive to a healthy team environment.

It is important to remember that some teams may encounter difficulties progressing from this stage. The presence of unresolved conflicts can lead to sabotage of individual and group objectives.

Creating an environment where it is safe for team members to express differing opinions and ideas is crucial, especially for those who are averse to conflict. Experienced team members can play a pivotal role in modeling positive team behavior, offering valuable guidance and examples for others to follow.

STAGE 3 | NORMING

During the norming stage, the team is at a critical juncture where they come together, align their perspectives, agree on the plan, establish clear timelines, and define each member's contributions based on their individual skills and expertise. This is a stage where some team members may need to let go of their own ideas and make sacrifices for the overall benefit of the team. It is also a time when mutual recognition of each other's strengths and acceptance of weaknesses start to emerge.

Trust becomes a cornerstone of this stage as team members actively seek help from one another, offer assistance, and build supportive relationships. It is also common for team members to socialize and bond with each other during this phase. While some conflict may still arise—especially during times of change or stress (storming)—the team is generally laying the foundation to work more effectively and cohesively.

The leader plays a crucial role in ensuring the team's success throughout the team development process, specifically:

Facilitating the "Norming" stage: The leader should take proactive steps to facilitate this stage by creating an environment that encourages open communication and collaboration. By providing guidance and support, the leader can help the team make collective decisions and develop the ability to work together cohesively. This can involve implementing structured team-building activities and conflict-resolution strategies to foster a sense of unity within the team.

Adopting a coaching approach: Rather than simply assigning tasks, the leader should focus on adopting a coaching style. This involves asking thought-provoking questions, providing constructive feedback, and offering guidance to empower team members to find their own solutions. By taking this approach, the leader can help team members build their capabilities and confidence, ultimately fostering a more self-sufficient and motivated team.

Organizing social events: To foster a strong sense of camaraderie and unity within the team, the leader should organize social events or activities outside of the typical work environment. These events provide opportunities for team members to socialize, bond, and build relationships beyond the scope of work-related tasks. By creating a relaxed and informal setting, the leader can help team members connect personally, which can significantly contribute to building a cohesive and harmonious team dynamic and ultimately prepare them to transition into the performing stage.

In the norming stage, raising concerns and new ideas can be challenging because everyone is eager to move past the uncertainty and unpleasantness of the "storming" phase. There's a push to progress and accomplish tasks, so leaders must stay open to new ideas and ensure that conflicts are addressed and resolved.

STAGE 4 | PERFORMING

In succinct terms, the team is currently at a stage where it is functioning effectively. The team has achieved stability and possesses clear, well-defined goals. At this stage, the team has established processes that are effective for the team, and team members adhere to them.

In addition, performing teams are able to carry out their tasks with minimal need for supervision and experience little to no conflict. Team members are highly motivated and demonstrate proficiency in completing tasks. Conflicts are no longer perceived as a threat, and the team recognizes the value of diverse perspectives. When a team reaches this stage, it can be characterized as a high-performing team.

As a leader, it is important to support a largely autonomous, high-performing team by delegating tasks efficiently, creating opportunities for the development of team members, and continuously articulating a clear vision for the team to align with. Additionally, a good leader should encourage healthy creative conflicts within the team and actively celebrate and reward achievements, thus empowering the team. It is crucial for the leader to recognize when the team is excelling and to step back to allow them to perform at their best.

CHAPTER 2

Recruiting the Right Players

"The team with the best players wins."

— Jack Welch

Many business owners and managers often ask, "Why is it so challenging to find committed and reliable individuals? Why don't my team members accomplish tasks according to my expectations?" Despite their best efforts, the strategies they've implemented, based on advice from sources such as books, magazines, and well-meaning acquaintances, don't seem to yield the desired results. This leaves them feeling frustrated and at a loss as to why their attempts at improvement haven't been successful.

If we remove the emotion from these questions and ask them in a way that could give us answers to improve our business, they would sound like this: "How can I find the right people for my business?" and "How can I get my people to do what I want and need them to do?" More than just emotional queries, these questions will lead us out of frustration and confusion and towards the systemic solutions we need.

Finding the right people for your business involves refining your recruiting and hiring processes, which is what this chapter is about. On the other hand, getting your people to do what you want—or more accurately, creating an environment where they want to do what you want them to do—is achieved through your entire management system. Both recruiting and hiring systems are essential to your management system because they are crucial in establishing a solid and productive relationship with new employees.

WHEN YOU FEEL THE URGE TO HIRE, DON'T! (AT LEAST, NOT YET...)

When considering hiring new people, start by asking yourself, "How can we achieve our goals without adding new staff?" Embrace the power of exploration and consider all possible approaches for achieving the desired outcome without hiring anyone. Only when you've exhausted all alternative options and determined that hiring is necessary should you begin the recruiting and hiring process.

As you build and grow your business, finding new people—the right people—will be one of the key processes within your people strategy. Sometimes, you'll need to replace employees who have left your company or retrain existing staff. And sometimes, you'll need to add new staff as you grow. In either case, having robust processes in place to recruit and hire new employees will add a pivotal element to your business that will serve you year after year, paving the way for a successful and sustainable future.

In this chapter, you'll learn a series of systems that will make up the way your company recruits and hires new employees. These systems will be leveraged to save you time and effort, and they'll be objective so that you will know that the decisions being made are the best ones possible.

PEOPLE AND SYSTEMS ARE THE KEY TO SUCCESS

The key to achieving your business goals lies in the collaboration between people and systems working together efficiently, harmoniously, and organically. Systems offer consistency, predictability, structure, and a benchmark for measuring outcomes. On the other hand, people contribute vitality, intelligence, creativity, innovation, discernment, judgment, reasoning, and humanity.

When making hiring decisions, it's essential to assess your needs objectively and determine the balance between a system-based approach and a people-based approach. Consider whether your existing team could handle the task with the right system in place. If they could, hiring may not be necessary. However, if they can't, then hiring becomes a priority.

If hiring is necessary, it's important to ask, "What specific responsibilities do we want this person to fulfill once hired? What is the day-to-day work of the position, and what are its long-term objectives?" In most cases, the new hire must be capable of executing the role's responsibilities and developing (or enhancing) the systems for carrying out those responsibilities.

The goal is to recruit individuals who are adept at both working in and on the job.

FINDING THE RIGHT PERSON FOR THE JOB

Once you've decided it's time to hire someone, the exciting part begins. The pressure to find the "right person" can be tough. After all, if you don't choose the right person, you'll end up hiring the wrong one. And no one wants that! We all know that a bad hiring decision can be costly in more ways than one, embarrassing, and a huge hassle.

So how will you recognize the "right person" for the job at your company?

Think of potential employees as a mix of what we know and what they don't know, related to the work they'll need to do and the results they'll need to achieve. Don't waste time trying to find the "perfect" person with every possible qualification for the job—that person doesn't exist. Your goal is to find a group of applicants with a good mix of what they do and don't know and then assess each one to find the best match for the position and your company.

Before delving into the specifics of a person's knowledge, it's important to assess whether a job applicant understands the distinction between what they know and what they don't. It's essential for employees to perceive themselves as a combination of their existing knowledge and areas where they need to learn more.

The ideal candidate for a job is someone who, regardless of their experience or achievements, views themselves as a beginner upon entering a new organization. A beginner is someone who is committed to lifelong learning, approaching each situation with an open mind and seeking knowledge, skills, insights, and wisdom from various sources. Employees who adopt a beginner's mindset consistently ask themselves, "What outcomes am I expected to achieve, and what do I know or need to learn to achieve the best results? How can I acquire and apply the necessary knowledge?" They recognize that they are at the beginning of a journey leading to greater accomplishments and contributions, and they embark on this path with enthusiasm.

Let's talk about the process of recruiting and hiring, something that you're probably familiar with—assessing what job applicants know and how it matches what you need. Each job requires specific capabilities, skills, interests, and knowledge. Your role is to identify these requirements and find the person who best matches them.

However, why do hiring mistakes seem to happen so often? The reality is that you may not have been truly evaluating these qualifications. While you may believe that you have, your beliefs and prejudices about the ideal candidate for a job may not align with reality.

The stereotypical pictures we create in our minds about the best salesperson, engineer, secretary, plumber, etc., are often based on our history, values, and past experiences. These stereotypes may not reflect what truly produces the best results for the position. Instead, we should focus on qualities and characteristics that generate the best results, rather than fitting a predetermined image.

To replace your current idea of the "right" person with a more accurate image, you need to remove yourself from the equation and allow the truth to emerge. Create a clear picture of the ideal person for each role in your business by defining the specific results you expect to achieve at each position. Assess the performance of your current employees and identify the traits and capabilities that set high performers apart. Use objective data and other relevant information to inform your evaluations. Continuously refine and document the qualifications required for each position over time.

RECRUITING AND HIRING EXHIBIT STRIKING PARALLELS WITH MARKETING AND SALES

There are a lot of similarities between the recruiting and hiring processes and your marketing and sales processes. In both cases, you're starting with a large, undifferentiated mass of unknown people—those people "out there" in the world. Your goal is to end up with a particular, distinct person who has an ongoing, mutually advantageous relationship with your company—an employee on the one hand, a customer on the other.

It is helpful to be aware of these similarities as you develop your recruiting and hiring systems because you can use the work you may have already done in marketing and sales to propel you forward. For example, the advertising messages you created to attract new customers may form part of the message you'll use to recruit employees. Your understanding of the "purchase decision chain" will help you pave the way for people to make one of the most important decisions in their lives—to become an employee of your company. And your awareness of how to engage with people to uncover what's under the surface will be invaluable in constructing your interview process.

IMPROVE YOUR DECISION-MAKING SKILLS

One of the most common pitfalls in making hiring decisions is relying on the "I have a good feeling about this person" syndrome.

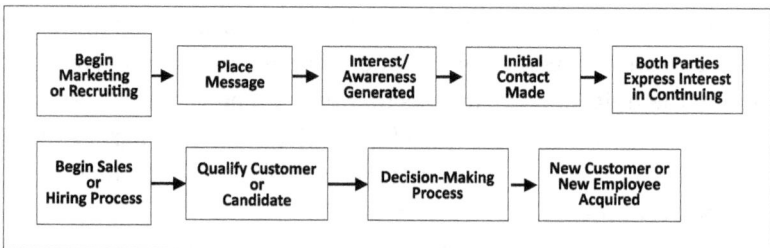

Begin Marketing or Recruiting	Place Message	Interest/ Awareness Generated	Initial Contact Made	Both Parties Express Interest in Continuing
Begin Sales or Hiring Process	Qualify Customer or Candidate	Decision-Making Process	New Customer or New Employee Acquired	

The similarity between recruiting and marketing effort.

When you have no clear criteria or objective standards for selection, the fallback is often "how you feel" or "your gut reaction." However, the process of bringing new employees into your company must go beyond just good or bad feelings. You need to develop recruiting and hiring systems that are as objective as possible, and then consider the feelings and gut reactions that shouldn't be ignored.

Clarity of thought and feeling leads to understanding, while confusion and distorted perceptions result from muddled thought and feeling.

By creating clear systems, your business will have the tools to confidently approach recruiting and hiring. You can start using these systems today and rely on them forever.

ANTICIPATE THE BEST OUTCOMES...YET REMAIN READY FOR LESS FAVORABLE ONES

Always remember: You'll soon be developing recruitment and hiring systems to bring a new level of objectivity and effectiveness to your business. This will involve creating action plans, recruitment messages, presentation scripts, interview questions, evaluation grids, and more. It will require focus, attention, and energy, but it will be worth every minute.

However, no matter how well these systems are designed, they won't guarantee that your employees will stay. In today's world, people are more likely than ever to change jobs, employers, industries, and even careers entirely.

This doesn't mean that you shouldn't strive to encourage your employees to stay for as long as possible or that you can't create an environment where people want to stay, grow, and contribute for many years. You certainly can and should. But when employee turnover does happen, you must be prepared for it. The best way to be prepared is by having orchestrated recruiting and hiring processes.

FIND PLAYERS FOR YOUR TEAM THAT ARE WORTH YOUR TIME

It is important to work on developing your recruiting and hiring systems when you don't urgently need to hire someone. This allows you to take a step back, gain a broader perspective, and be as objective as possible. Instead of viewing recruiting and hiring as a response to an immediate need in your business, consider it in relation to the overall goals and operation of your business.

Think about what the people in your business are here to do: They are here to participate in your business's central mission and values. Your business has a purpose, a logic, and a set of guidelines. These elements should be reflected in your recruiting and hiring process, as they set your business apart and ensure that every employee is fully engaged because they understand and are committed to the objectives of your business.

Instead of waiting until after they become employees, give every person who comes to work in your business the opportunity to make an informed choice. Make sure they understand the principles and goals behind the work they're being asked to do.

When developing your recruiting and hiring systems, keep in mind that you're not just looking for employees; you're looking for individuals who are aligned with your business's purpose.

You're seeking people who are looking for more than just a job and who understand that the best way to do their job is a reflection of who they are. This is the message you should communicate as you recruit and hire, and it's essential to convey this early in the process.

By creating effective recruiting and hiring systems, you'll build a solid foundation for your company, which will help you navigate both employee turnover and company growth. This way, when you need to bring in new people, for any reason, you'll have a reliable system already in place to do it effectively.

CHAPTER 3

Hire Slow, Fire Fast!

"People are not your most important asset. The right people are."

— Jim Collins

Many companies tend to hire quickly but are slow to let go of underperforming employees. The pressure for rapid growth often makes leaders rush the hiring process while avoiding the difficult task of addressing poor performance. This approach can result in what Guy Kawasaki, during his time at Apple, referred to as the "bozo explosion."

The rapid expansion of a Silicon Valley company led to uncontrolled growth, ultimately resulting in a large-scale layoff. The experience was akin to performing open-heart surgery on the organization. Rather than upholding a Lean and entrepreneurial team through consistent discipline, the company's leaders permitted the organization's vital processes to become obstructed, leading to the failure of significant systems. As a result, they had to resort to extensive corrective measures that traumatized the entire company.

When we compare this behavior with that of a 700-person company that generates over a billion dollars in annual revenue, we can observe a remarkable ratio of $1.4 million in revenue per employee. This ratio reflects the careful and strategic approach to achieving such impressive financial performance.

KEEPING ONE PERSON IS NOT COMPASSIONATE

In today's world, where youth unemployment is a prevalent issue, the principle of "hire slow, fire fast" may come across as unsympathetic. However, upon closer examination, I believe this approach is ultimately more caring for three specific reasons.

First, creating organizations with excessive bureaucracy and inefficiency that are destined to fail in the long run is not a beneficial outcome for anyone. Instead, what we truly need are robust, sustainable companies that can weather the challenges of the future and provide stable employment opportunities.

Second, keeping one person isn't compassionate; it makes the whole team struggle. We need teams in which everyone can trust each other to do a great job. If "hire slow, fire fast" sounds harsh or mercurial, consider how harsh it is to allow a whole team to be held hostage by someone who should not have been hired in the first place. And while we're on the subject, lacking courage is not the same as having compassion.

Third, attempting to compel someone to fulfill a role that does not align with their true abilities and nature is ultimately unsustainable and lacks compassion. Continuously subjecting an individual to the same negative feedback, week after week, month after month, or year after year, while keeping them in the wrong position is detrimental and doesn't serve their best interests. As the poet Mary Oliver so eloquently puts it, "Each person's life is unique and precious, and it deserves to be honored as such."

While it is beneficial to explore whether the person can be well-placed within the company in a more suitable role, it's essential to acknowledge that simply reassigning them is not the definitive solution if they are genuinely mismatched for their current position. Merely transferring the individual to a different part of the organization only displaces the problem and does not address the underlying issue.

The "hire slow, fire fast" approach to hiring involves taking a very careful and thorough approach to selecting new employees, while also being quick to part ways with those who are not the right fit for the company.

I contend your company should be known for utilizing a highly selective approach to hiring. Strive to identify candidates who naturally align with the company's values and culture. In the hiring process, your team should conduct numerous interviews and also have potential hires spend a day working alongside the team. This allows both the company and the candidate to experience each other in a natural setting, providing a more accurate and comprehensive understanding before any commitments are made.

For example, a client of mine recently had a job candidate assist with a sign project installation. Although he was skilled at the task, at the end of the day, he carelessly threw his tools into a box instead of putting them away correctly. When they discussed this incident with the project manager, everyone agreed that this behavior was an obvious reason not to hire the candidate.

If that might seem overly strict, you might not want to work for such a company. However, that is the intention. Your standards for hiring should be so high that many people would prefer not to work for you. You want to attract only a select few who are the right fit rather than appealing to the masses. This author believes it's better to be short-staffed than to hire the wrong person.

It is important to recognize that for this particular approach to be practical, it is crucial to handle the process of letting employees go in a humane manner. The term "firing" often carries a connotation of harshness and humiliation, but it is important to understand that it doesn't have to be this way. It is possible to part ways with employees in a respectful manner, treating them with dignity and kindness rather than making them feel like criminals or disrespecting them in any way.

When a leader in the sign manufacturing industry realized she had made a hiring mistake, she could have tried to hide her error and force the fit through endless rounds of feedback and a painful performance improvement plan. However, in this case, the problem was a basic personality clash. The employee was more aggressive than the company culture and abrasive to everyone on the team, making it challenging to resolve the issue.

After observing the new hire's impact on her team for just two weeks, she decided to have a conversation with the employee. She expressed that she didn't think the company culture was the right fit and suggested that it would be best to part ways. Despite this conversation, the team, including the departing employee, went out for drinks that evening. Additionally, the company offered free career coaching to help the employee find a better fit elsewhere.

We can enhance the overall quality of talent within our organizations by embracing the concept of "talent density," as advocated by Reed Hastings, the CEO of Netflix. This means taking a deliberate and meticulous approach to the hiring process, ensuring that we bring in individuals who not only possess the necessary skills but also align with the organization's values and culture.

Additionally, it involves being swift to address any mismatches or performance issues, which may require having challenging conversations and demonstrating strong leadership. While executing this approach may present its challenges, the long-term benefits for the individuals, teams, and organizations involved are substantial.

CHAPTER 4

Developing Your Team

"Take care of your employees and they'll take care of your business."

— Richard Branson

The principle of business systemization is to maximize performance, which is good and necessary. However, it's important to clarify that, even if you've created highly sophisticated systems, you still need qualified, committed employees not only to use those systems but also to improve them. This work is ongoing.

Systems are not designed to eliminate the human touch from your company. Rather, they free you and your employees from daily concerns such as, "How do we make a sale today? How do we process new orders? How do we request supplies?" Your systems provide the answers to these questions.

With systems in place, everyone can focus their creative energies on "How can we do it better?" rather than "How do we do it?"

Employee development is not a one-time task but an ongoing process. It's about creating a workplace where people are self-motivated, feel valued, and constantly strive to exceed their own limits.

Systems development is actually the easier part of business development. When it comes to people development, get ready to face some exciting challenges.

WE ARE MORE SIMILAR THAN DIFFERENT

Remember: People are people, including your employees. They have their own goals and aspirations that need to align with your company's. They want recognition, rewards, and opportunities for growth. To attract and retain quality employees, you need to address their needs and become an effective mentor.

UNDERSTANDING THE TRUE MEANING OF MENTORING

Have you ever found yourself staying up late, trying to figure out how to motivate your people and make them more productive? You're not alone. Many managers believe that increasing salaries, improving the work environment, or throwing parties will automatically boost morale and productivity. However, our experience has shown that true motivation comes from within. It is a self-initiated drive that must already exist within individuals. To truly understand what motivates your team, you'll need to expand beyond your current role and become a mentor who coaches and guides people to be their best. By creating an environment that allows people to be productive and fulfilled, highly motivated individuals will be eager to work for you.

THE EMPLOYEE DEVELOPMENT MEETING IS AN OPPORTUNITY FOR MENTORING

One effective way to mentor and coach your employees and create a highly motivating, productive environment is through the Employee

Development meeting. Managers hold this meeting weekly with each of their reporting employees. It is done individually and face-to-face and is scheduled in advance as a top priority for everyone's work week.

This meeting should not be held sporadically or only when there's a problem. When conducted regularly and consistently across your company, it will become the backbone of your management system.

The Employee Development meeting is:

- A forum for discussion, problem-solving, conflict resolution, and planning that leaves your employees feeling listened to and empowered to take action.
- A routine time to discuss current work in order to make agreements for work to be accomplished, prioritize and discuss any exceptions, exchange substantive information, clarify procedures and results, and conduct other follow-up related to current work.
- A coaching session that helps people stay on a productive track.
- An opportunity to guide your people toward their personal and professional objectives so their experience in your business becomes more positive and meaningful.
- A way to recognize people as individuals, not just as successful employees.
- Most of all, it is the vehicle for helping every person in your company face and overcome the real-life issues that get in the way of being the best they can be. Imagine the power and impact of the meeting that creates true growth for each and every employee, as well as better results for the business!

How will you find time for these meetings? Don't worry—time will find you because Employee Development meetings are time-savers.

Employee Development meetings help reduce daily interruptions. Since your employees know they have weekly time with you, you can encourage them to save most problems and questions until then. No more knocking on your door or taking time from others with unnecessary interruptions.

Employee Development meetings follow an agenda to keep the meeting focused. You and your employees identify important areas to be discussed beforehand. When you come to the meeting, you've both done your homework. You know what topics need to be covered. No time is wasted on tangents or irrelevant issues.

These meetings provide specific recommendations for follow-up. Whether your employees are having difficulty with a work activity or reacting negatively to a new policy, you have an opportunity to address these issues before they become serious problems. You will be able to create appropriate plans with them to eliminate any obstacles in their way – saving time and energy for both of you!

Similarly, you can praise them for their accomplishments, provide guidance on new skills, or assist them in aligning their personal objectives with the company's goals.

Employee Development meetings facilitate individual growth and the ability to make informed decisions. One of the most common challenges faced by business owners and managers is the perception that their employees' decision-making does not align with their own, resulting in choices and decisions that are often subpar or entirely unacceptable.

These meetings provide an excellent opportunity to address mistakes and errors constructively, using them as valuable teaching moments to guide employees towards making increasingly better decisions, both in their professional and personal interactions.

Regardless of the desired outcome, Employee Development meetings bring you and your employees closer to creating a rewarding and motivating work environment that is often sought after but rarely achieved. It is definitely a worthwhile investment of your time.

SUBSTANCE AND SPIRIT

You must understand and integrate both the substance of the Employee Development meeting and the spirit of it. Either one without the other won't work.

Substance refers to the actual content of your Employee Development meetings. Spirit means taking on a new picture of what it means to be a manager and a mentor: one who recognizes that the role is to get results through other people and that the way to do this is to be a true mentor who helps people move beyond their limitations to be the best they can possibly be.

Every manager in your company must strive to embody this model— both the substance of it and the spirit of it.

A MEETING WHERE EVERYONE WINS!

It is widely acknowledged that business meetings can be a significant waste of time, money, and energy. Many managers struggle to conduct productive meetings, and as a result, employees often leave feeling more frustrated than when they arrived. It is also common for the relationship between employees and their managers to feel more like a formality than a meaningful exchange, and often, it can be more intrusive than liberating. However, it doesn't have to be this way.

By embracing the "manager as mentor" model and utilizing the agendas and techniques for Employment Development meetings, every manager can empower their employees to transcend limitations and reach their fullest potential. Managers can act as coaches, guiding their team to handle challenges constructively and creating an environment that addresses employees' needs for recognition, meaningful work, and personal and professional growth.

These efforts will yield significant returns for the managers, the employees, and the company as a whole. A company that fosters such an environment will become a place where people at every level are eager to work, rather than feeling obligated to do so.

CHAPTER 5

Position Agreements

"The discipline of writing something down is the first step toward making it happen."

— Lee Iacocca

What are your employees doing throughout the day? How are they using their time? Are they fulfilling their job responsibilities? What exactly are you compensating them for?

In the midst of our busy daily lives, it's easy to forget that everyone in the business is there to achieve one goal: to produce results. Therefore, one of the most impactful efforts you can make in your business is to establish systems to support people in producing their best results.

Assuming the responsibility to deliver tangible outcomes is fundamental for every individual within your company; whether consciously acknowledged or not, this responsibility begins the very day they join the organization. Position agreements serve to explicitly outline and define the essential nature of this responsibility, empowering individuals to take control of their roles and responsibilities.

IT'S ALL ABOUT ACCOUNTABILITY

The position agreement is a comprehensive document that outlines the specific responsibilities, expectations, and objectives for each employee within the company. It serves as a guideline for employees to understand their roles and how to achieve the desired results. Some companies provide their employees with "job descriptions" during the hiring process or on their first day of work. However, a job description only scratches the surface in terms of outlining the full scope of an employee's role and responsibilities, often resembling a basic checklist of tasks.

Position agreements are not just written agreements between managers and the employees who report to them. They are agreements between responsible adults, grounded in mutual respect and a clear understanding of what needs to be accomplished. This mutual understanding and respect is the foundation of these agreements that outline the employee's accountabilities, which the employee agrees to and the manager agrees to support the employee.

How does a position agreement help employees be accountable for achieving the results of their position? It does so by capturing three specific elements in a clear and organized manner:

Result statement: Explains why the employee's position exists in the company.

Work listing: Specifies the exact work required to produce the result.

Standards: Describes how the work should be performed.

Often, a job description is just a document kept on file in the personnel office to meet the legal requirements of labor laws. When it's actually used on the job, it's usually just a formality or a demand from a superior to a subordinate. A job description isn't really an agreement, and it contains a lot of irrelevant information that doesn't really help anyone achieve anything. It lacks a results-oriented approach that keeps people focused on the right things. Your employees deserve better. They need a real tool that will help them understand what it means to be accountable.

Accountability is an interesting concept. When you have accountability, you're responsible for producing a result. You can either do the work yourself to achieve the result or delegate some or all of the work to someone who reports to you. When you delegate in this way, you haven't given up your accountability— you've created a new accountability for someone else. Your employee is now accountable for producing a certain result associated with the work items you've delegated. However, you still remain accountable for the overall result. This concept is clearly reflected in the results statements written in conjunction with your company's organization chart, where each employee's result contributes to or is a part of the result at the next level, ultimately aligning with your company's strategic objective.

LINKING YOUR PEOPLE TO YOUR VISION

Your strategic objective communicates the future direction of your business. It influences your organizational strategy and the business systems your organization will operate. Position agreements place your employees within this vision, clarifying their roles in the organization, specifying the business systems they are responsible for, and outlining the results they are expected to achieve.

Position agreements connect everyone in your organization directly to your strategic objective—from top to bottom and across the organization. The person at the top (such as the president or chief executive officer) is ultimately responsible for achieving the strategic objective.

The tasks and responsibilities needed to achieve the strategic objective are identified and assigned to senior managers, who then delegate them to lower-level positions, creating a chain of accountability throughout the organizational chart. This ensures that everyone is responsible for delivering results that directly contribute to the company's success, and there is no evasion of responsibility. Nobody can pass on their responsibilities and then disregard them. Each individual carries out their own tasks, oversees the work of their subordinates, and reports their results to their superiors. The ties that bind the organization into a cohesive whole (rather than a disjointed group of employees) are the position agreements.

There is no room for uncertainty, misunderstanding, or doubt. Every employee with a position agreement knows precisely what they need to achieve and how to accomplish it. This level of clarity is invaluable. It establishes a professional and productive working environment while fostering warm and respectful relationships. It puts your employees on the right path to contribute directly and effectively to your vision for the future of your business.

POSITION AGREEMENTS ARE NOT NEGOTIABLE

A position agreement is shaped by the owners' vision for the business, the systems the business operates as it serves its customers, and the organizational strategy. It cannot be the result of give-and-take negotiations between managers and employees based on their personal needs and preferences. It defines a position based on the needs of the business to produce results that contribute to the greater purpose.

Position agreements are not set in stone. They must be revised periodically to respond to changing circumstances as the business grows and adapts to its markets. Employees who occupy the positions are often the first ones to detect the need for change and make specific suggestions in that regard. It's all part of the innovation that's part and parcel of a business that works.

Changes in position agreements over time are the result of cooperation and agreement between managers and employees. However, the manager has the accountability for making the decision to change the position agreement. It's not put to a vote; It's decided upon by the manager. The process is one of exchanging ideas and fully discussing alternatives until it is time for the manager to make the decision. Then, no compromises, no votes, no shaping the position to the individual's tastes and personal needs. The decision is made by the manager based on the needs of the business, and the employee agrees to the revised position agreement. If not, there is a reassignment or an amicable parting of the ways—two adults making rational decisions.

WHAT MAKES UP AN EFFECTIVE POSITION AGREEMENT?

The position agreement is a written document consisting of five parts:

Position Identification: This section includes the title of the position, the title of the manager's position to which this position reports, and the titles of any positions reporting to it. This helps to place the position within the organization chart, showing its hierarchy within the organization. The section also includes the results statements of the positions reporting to this position, along with their titles. This is important for a manager to be aware of the results they are supporting their employees to achieve.

Result Statement: This should clearly outline the results expected from this position and align with the result statement established for the position during the development of the Organizational Strategy.

Work Listing: This should provide a detailed list of the tasks and responsibilities associated with the position. It includes both strategic and tactical work, and each work item listed should outline the process for completing it.

Standards: These are the requirements for achieving the desired result and performing the work. This includes specifications for quantity, quality, and behavior. When setting standards, consider what works and what doesn't work for the employee in this role.

Signatures: Both the manager and the employee filling the position must sign the position agreement. This signifies the employee's commitment to achieve the desired result in line with the set work and standards, and the manager's commitment to support the employee. While the employee is ultimately accountable, the position agreement promotes a team approach and discourages an "us versus them" mindset. All position agreements have these same elements, and the development of your company's position agreements should be orchestrated so the format and language conventions are used consistently.

There are variations in position agreements, each with unique content. For non-managers, since they do not have other positions reporting to them, their position agreements will not list the titles and outcomes of any reporting positions. Therefore, you should exclude the "reporting positions" section entirely from your position agreement template for non-managerial positions. Another key difference lies in the distribution of strategic and tactical work.

POSITION AGREEMENTS MEAN COMMITMENT

Position agreements are important documents that go beyond mere paperwork or one-way mandates directed at employees. While not legally binding, they are morally binding and represent a philosophy and approach to business.

At their best, they reflect how people throughout an organization can collaborate to fulfill their responsibilities and experience the satisfaction of personal success. They prioritize outcomes over mere activity and are instrumental in guiding your employees towards achieving your vision in the most efficient manner.

With position agreements in place, you won't need to ensure that your employees are simply staying "busy," as they will be engaged in meaningful and productive work that truly contributes to the success of your business!

CHAPTER 6

Functional Cross-Training

"It is not enough to be busy... The question is: what are we busy about?"

— Henry David Thoreau

When I'm called upon to assist shop owners in rejuvenating their businesses, they often take pride in their efforts to cross-train their workforce and implement robust production scheduling practices. However, it's disheartening to see these same businesses, despite their best efforts, grappling with common challenges such as decreased profitability, cash flow issues, delayed deliveries, excessive overtime, and rework.

The most common mistake among shop managers is failing to recognize the value of properly balancing shop talent to maximize productivity. This balance is not just about workload distribution; it's about tapping into the underutilized capacity to enhance bottom-line profits without the need for additional manpower investments. Understanding and implementing this balance is crucial for the success of your business. Once you grasp this concept, you'll see your business in a new light.

PROMOTE GOOD SINGLE-TASKING

Before I discuss these productivity strategies, I want to address the misconception about multitasking.

How frequently have you encountered individuals proudly proclaiming, "I'm a great multitasker?" Many people wear this as a badge of honor. This may be okay for a customer service representative or receptionist, but in the shop, it is disastrous!

It's important to consider the actual implications of multitasking. Traditionally, multitasking involves the simultaneous execution of multiple tasks. However, it is worth noting that even computers can't really multitask. Instead, they process information at such incredibly high speeds that they create the illusion of multitasking.

When it comes to multitasking, it's crucial to understand that there are two distinct types: one that is beneficial and another that can be detrimental.

At the Goldratt Institute, I learned about "good single-tasking," which prioritizes focusing on one task at a time for optimal production efficiency. This is in contrast to "bad multitasking," which is commonly practiced in many shops and leads to reduced efficiency.

In a multi-job shop environment, it is common for resources to switch between tasks on different jobs or within the same job to show progress, as often occurs when an owner must report to a customer that a job is on schedule when it's actually not.

This type of multitasking often increases the duration of all jobs and is generally considered bad multitasking. However, if a worker is required to stop a lower priority task in order to complete a higher priority task, thus helping to complete that job earlier, it is generally considered good single-tasking.

Prioritizing and focusing on one task at a time is crucial for ensuring that projects are completed promptly and efficiently. Good single-tasking promotes a steady and uninterrupted workflow and is essential for safeguarding profitability. Conversely, engaging in bad multitasking can result in higher costs due to frequent interruptions and the possibility of errors, which may necessitate additional effort to rectify, as emphasized in earlier sections. Therefore, adopting the motto "Prioritize and Single Task!" is vital to maximize productivity and quality.

FUNCTIONAL CROSS-TRAINING IS KEY

Cross-training can be very beneficial because it enables employees to develop skills in multiple areas, creating more value for themselves and the company. However, it can also have drawbacks if employees are trained in areas that are not operationally relevant. The key is to focus on "functional" cross-training.

The term "functional" refers to adding new capabilities to a system and then using those capabilities to enhance productivity. As I mentioned earlier, to achieve maximum throughput, managers should focus on optimizing their system's performance before attempting to fully maximize their team's potential. Once the system is operating at its peak efficiency, managers can identify specific cross-training programs to further enhance their team's ability to complete additional work. This approach comprehensively evaluates the system's capabilities and provides a strategic method for increasing overall productivity.

Before commencing your training, ensuring that all your systems function optimally is essential. Once you are prepared to initiate the training, you will be required to develop your Shop Talent Index and identify the "who" and the "what." The "who" represents your team members, while the "what" encompasses the products, skills, and standard operating procedures (SOPs).

EVALUATING YOUR TEAM

Employees are categorized into skill levels based on their proficiency in carrying out specific tasks. In this example, a five-tiered scale is used, consisting of the following levels:

LEVEL 1—Novice | A novice is an entry-level person who is new or inexperienced. They gain practical knowledge through apprenticing under a Level 3 or 4 Associate and learning from challenging experiences.

LEVEL 2—Advanced Beginner | An advanced beginner is someone who has acquired some knowledge or skill in a particular area but has not yet reached the point where they can complete taskwork without close supervision or understanding the interrelated components of the whole production process.

LEVEL 3—Competent | Competent individuals are those who have acquired the essential skills, knowledge, training, and experience to perform tasks effectively without the need for coaching or instruction. This capability allows them to carry out their responsibilities with confidence.

LEVEL 4—Proficient | A proficient worker is someone who has honed advanced skills and expertise in a specific area through extensive training, practical experience, and continuous learning; their speed and accuracy make them good candidates to perform as a team leader.

LEVEL 5—Expert | An expert is recognized when they have demonstrated comprehensive mastery in multiple disciplines, achieved through at least 10 years of committed experience. They are equipped with the qualifications and skills necessary to instruct and guide others effectively in their respective areas of expertise.

SHOP TALENT INDEX

The Shop Talent Index (STI) is essential for evaluating and managing the workforce training program. It serves as a key component in optimizing production efficiency and output. The STI is closely interconnected with the production work-in-progress (WIP) schedule, which plays a vital role in effective production management. In the following sections of this book, we will delve into the intricacies of the production management process and the coordinated use of the STI and WIP schedule to enhance overall productivity and performance.

To efficiently manage your workforce and production process, consider creating a comprehensive chart outlining all the tasks necessary for producing your products (listed horizontally) and your workers' skills (listed vertically). You can then assess and score the proficiency of each worker in relation to the specific tasks. By doing so, you'll be able to pinpoint any skill gaps within your departments and identify areas that require additional training or development. This allows for a more in-depth analysis of your workforce's capabilities and ensures that you're able to address any skill deficiencies effectively.

There are six steps to setting up your STI:

Step 1: Create your Shop Talent Index.

To get started, open a spreadsheet application such as Excel and create a series of rows to organize your data effectively. The first three rows should be dedicated to (1.) Resource Name, (2.) Primary Responsibility, and (3.) Skill Level, to clearly establish the key information for each resource. Following this, you can include additional rows to provide task IDs, categorizing them within designated sections for each department. This helps to effectively represent workstations, machines, or action steps within your manufacturing process and ensures alignment with your standard operating procedures (SOPs) and production WIP scheduling system.

ACME COMPANY - SHOP TALENT INDEX (STI)

RESOURCE NAME	PRIMARY DEPARTMENT	SKILL RATING	CNC	Drill	Shear	Weld	Bond	Rout	Grind	Assemble	Prep	Prime	Mix	Paint	Plotter	Printer 1	Laser 2	Weed	Apply	Assemble
			FABRICATION								PAINT				GRAPHICS					
		TASK CODE	F.1	F.2	F.3	F.4	F.5	F.6	F.7	F.8	P.1	P.2	P.3	P.4	G.1	G.2	G.3	G.4	G.5	G.6
Randy Pierce	GRAPHICS	4.0													5.0	5.0	3.0	4.0	4.0	3.0
Jason McKinny	GRAPHICS	3.0													2.0	2.0	2.0	4.0	4.0	4.0
Alice Crabbe	GRAPHICS	1.8													1.0	1.0	1.0	4.0	2.0	2.0
Ryan Channing	FAB	3.3	1.0	1.0	4.0	4.0	4.0	4.0	4.0	4.0										
Bill James	FAB	3.0	2.0	3.0	3.0	1.0	3.0	4.0	4.0	4.0										
Harry Curren	PAINT	4.3									4.0	4.0	4.0	5.0						
Jim Mason	PAINT	2.3									2.0	2.0	2.0	3.0						
Sandy Wong	INSTALL	3.8																		
John Peterson	INSTALL	2.8																		
		SCORE	3.0	4.0	7.0	5.0	7.0	8.0	8.0	8.0	6.0	6.0	6.0	8.0	8.0	8.0	6.0	12.0	10.0	9.0

[1. Novice, 2. Advanced Beginner, 3. Competent, 4. Proficient, 5. Expert]

Step 2: Evaluate Your Talent.

During this phase, we will conduct a comprehensive evaluation of the team's capabilities and limitations. To accomplish this, we will individually assess each team member on a scale of one to five in terms of their accuracy, speed, competence, experience, and craftsmanship.

It's important to note that this assessment is not purely quantitative, as much of the insight will be gained through direct collaboration with the team on the shop floor. By observing and understanding their unique talents, passions, and personalities, we aim to create a holistic assessment that goes beyond just numerical ratings.

Step 3: Analyze the Data.

As we move forward, it's crucial to focus on converting the data we've gathered and creating a graphical representation based on the Pareto principle. This principle, also known as the 80/20 rule, suggests that 80 percent of the benefits or results come from 20 percent of the efforts or causes. It also indicates that 80 percent of the problems can be attributed to 20 percent of the causes.

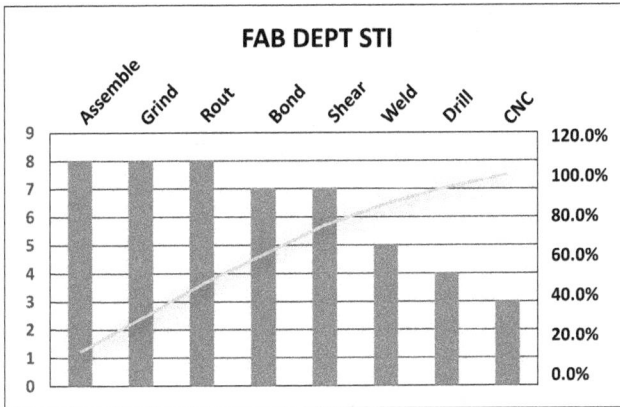

FAB DEPT STI

By conducting a Pareto Analysis, we can precisely identify the areas or tasks that will have the most significant impact and payoff, enabling us to prioritize and direct our efforts in the most productive manner.

Step 4: Assess the WIP and Sales Forecast.

After conducting a thorough analysis of your current situation, you have identified the specific resources that are currently lacking. This information is up-to-date and takes into account all relevant factors.

However, we need to prepare for ongoing activities within the sales department. It's important to gain insight into whether there are plans to assign a significant amount of work that our team may not be adequately prepared to handle at this time.

To obtain this information, it is essential to analyze additional data sets. These may include the sales forecast, the historical record of annual trends and seasonal variations, and the job status report (JSR), which I will discuss in upcoming chapters.

Step 5: Identify Your Constraints.

In the specific example, only the fabrication department is shown, and it's apparent that the weakest area is in the CNC shop.

It's important not to jump to conclusions prematurely before completing your analysis, as this may not accurately indicate where training and recruiting efforts need to be focused. Nonetheless, this area offers room for improvement for the shop and growth opportunities for employees.

The choice cannot be random; you'll experience problems downstream if you guess wrong.

Step 6: Implement Your Training Agenda.

Training plays a crucial role in shaping your organization's productivity and performance. Training equips employees with comprehensive knowledge of their roles and the necessary skills to carry out their responsibilities effectively. This, in turn, enhances their confidence levels, positively impacting their overall job performance. The following narrative will help you put your training agenda together:

Identify your goals and outcomes. Figure out what you want to achieve and what you want your participants to learn, do, or feel by the end of the session. Also, consider how you will measure their progress and success. Write down your goals and outcomes in SMART (Specific, Measurable, Achievable, Relevant, and Time-bound) terms and use them as the foundation of your agenda.

Break down your content into chunks. Chunking is a powerful technique for organizing your material into meaningful and manageable units based on criteria such as topic, difficulty level, or activity type. By using chunking, you can prevent overwhelming your participants with too much information and create a coherent flow of content that aligns with your objectives and desired outcomes.

Assign time and resources to each chunk. Time is a valuable and limited resource in any training session, so estimating how much time you'll need for each section and making adjustments as necessary is important. Additionally, you should consider the resources required to present each section of content, such as slides, handouts, videos, or equipment. It's crucial to ensure that you have enough time and resources to effectively deliver your content and accommodate various learning styles and preferences.

Write and format your agenda. Your agenda should include a title, a summary, a list of goals and outcomes, a schedule with time and resource allocations, and any participant instructions or reminders. Use headings, bullet points, colors, fonts, and icons to make it visually appealing and easy to read. Keep it concise enough to fit on one page yet detailed enough to provide a clear overview of your training session.

WHY TRAINING RECORDS MATTER

Keeping accurate training records is essential for promoting safe and efficient work. Proper records management allows organizations to anticipate training needs and fulfill all legal requirements. This helps to maintain regulatory compliance with local, state, and federal agencies, which is particularly crucial for manufacturers to avoid unnecessary downtime and increased administrative costs due to noncompliance.

Even if training records are not a regulatory necessity, internal management should track employee training. Establishing guidelines proactively ensures compliance and provides a benchmark for performance evaluations. These records are especially valuable for assessing the effectiveness of training programs.

You now should have the necessary knowledge and skills to attract the employees who will help you operate your business successfully for years to come.

CHAPTER 7

Lean Production Philosophy

"Give me a place to stand, and I can move the earth."

—Archimedes

At the turn of the 20th century, the concept of "Lean" had not yet been named, but the elimination of waste had developed from a method used by a small number of influential individuals to a popular movement. Lean would undergo significant developments during these years. The introduction of process analysis and process mapping by certain individuals, as well as the incorporation of scientific management to enhance manufacturing processes, would play significant roles in the development of Lean.

THE GILBRETHS: ADVANCING MANUFACTURING EFFICIENCY

A significant advancement in Lean history occurred thanks to the contributions of an influential woman named Lillian Gilbreth. She was a remarkable figure with diverse expertise, functioning as a psychologist, industrial engineer, educator, businesswoman, and consultant. Lillian was a trailblazer in applying psychology to time and motion studies. In 1915, she became one of the first female engineers to earn a Ph.D.

Additionally, she held the distinction of being the first industrial or organizational psychologist. These achievements solidified her status as a pioneering figure in the realm of business psychology.

Lillian married her husband, Frank, in 1904. They worked together, until he died in 1924, evaluating the effects of human factors on the efficiency of production processes. Lillian focused on studying the motivations of workers and the effects of employees' attitudes on the outcome of processes, while Frank focused on the logistical side—specifically, how the reduction of human motion could increase the efficiency of assembly processes.

After studying construction and factory workers, Frank and Lillian created charts and maps that showed the steps needed to complete a product or achieve a result. These diagrams included details like cycle time, inventory, and equipment information. By using these visual outlines, the Gilbreths could differentiate between wasteful activities and those that added value. This method is known today as process mapping, process charting, or value stream mapping.

While Eiji Toyota is often credited with developing this process shortly after World War II, the true credit belongs to Lillian and Frank Gilbreth. They are also credited with originating the concept of eliminating waste, a primary tenet of Lean manufacturing. Although innovators throughout Lean history focused on efficiency and process improvement, the Gilbreths first defined these activities as eliminating waste, which later came to define Lean.

HENRY FORD: EXPANDING CONCEPTS FOR MASS PRODUCTION

In 1891, Henry Ford began working as an engineer at the Edison Illuminating Company of Detroit. He successfully constructed his first working gasoline engine in 1893, and by 1896, he had produced his first vehicle. Known as the Ford Quadricycle, it was built using the frame of a horse buggy, four bicycle wheels, and a gasoline engine.

Later in the same year, Ford had the opportunity to meet Thomas Edison, who was greatly impressed with his designs and encouraged Ford to continue his work. By 1898, Ford had completed his second vehicle and resigned from the Edison Illuminating Company to pursue his work full-time.

Ford founded his first automobile company with funding from Detroit lumber baron William H. Murphy in 1899. However, the company failed within three years. He then formed a second automobile company called the Henry Ford Company in 1901 and left it within a year when Murphy brought in a consultant named Henry M. Leland. Initially planned for liquidation, they decided to reorganize the company instead, leading Ford to depart and the Henry Ford Company to become the Cadillac Automobile Company.

On June 16, 1903, Ford established the Ford Motor Company with $28,000 in capital from a group of shareholders that included the Dodge brothers. His objective was to create a vehicle that was affordable to the masses. On October 1, 1908, the Model T was introduced, priced at $825 (equivalent to about $23,000 today).

In 1910, the Ford Motor Company relocated its operations to Highland Park, Michigan, known as the "birthplace of Lean manufacturing." Here, Ford and a group of talented engineers and mechanics experimented with production methods, layouts, and material handling processes to streamline their operations. Through the implementation of Lean manufacturing practices (standardizing processes, implementing continuous flow, and incorporating advanced machining techniques), they reduced assembly time from 12 hours per vehicle to under three hours. As a result, the vehicle price steadily decreased every year, and demand skyrocketed. By 1920, most Americans were driving a Model T.

Henry Ford began his involvement with the concept of interchangeability while planning the production of his Model N automobile. He believed that interchangeability was essential in increasing production output. He also decided it was important to simplify operations. In order to facilitate interchangeability and simplification, one of Ford's mechanics built new machines that were simple enough for anyone to successfully produce a high-quality result.

After these developments, there were just a few final steps before the famous Ford assembly line could be implemented. First, Ford and his team set up machine tools in the order of their operation and installed gravity slides for the quick movement of parts from one stage of assembly to the next. However, the most important step was simplifying tasks enough for unskilled laborers. Once this was done, the first Ford assembly line came alive, and workers would move from station to station to complete each part.

However, some workers could move more quickly than others, so Ford needed to regulate production speed. The best way to do this was to control the speed of the assembly line instead of employees' speed. The assembly line cut the overall assembly time for a Model T engine by more than 50 percent. By 1913, Ford was producing 200,000 automobiles per year.

Despite the grandeur of the Ford Motor Company, there were numerous problems. One of the primary issues was retaining employees. Ford's production relied on a labor force that was so desperate for money and employment that workers would compromise their dignity and self-esteem for a mere five dollars an hour. They would conduct mass interviews and hire hundreds of people, knowing that many would leave by the end of the day.

It wasn't until the 1920s, with the rise of labor unions, that employees had a platform to voice their concerns about poor treatment and working conditions. During the same period, the automobile industry was rapidly expanding. In order to remain competitive, Ford would need to introduce new models annually in various colors. However, the Ford assembly line was not easily adaptable to this level of flexibility.

At the time, General Motors, a major competitor to Ford, saw this as an opportunity to overtake the market. Alfred P. Sloan, a key figure at General Motors, recognized that Ford's production practices were the key to achieving this. Sloan developed business and manufacturing strategies focused on high-volume production and variety. By the mid-1930s, Sloan and General Motors had surpassed Ford and established dominance in the automotive industry.

Despite all of this, many Lean production concepts utilized by Ford became integral parts of the growth of the automotive industry, allowing Ford to maintain his fame. In fact, Ford's methods of production, in conjunction with Taylorism, were a deciding factor in the Allied victory of World War II.

TOYOTA ENTERS THE LEAN VERNACULAR

After WW II, Eiji Toyota was confronted with formidable financial, technological, and labor relations challenges. Eiji Toyota and his production genius, Taichi Ohno, recognized that traditional mass production methods would not suit Japan. They responded to these obstacles by devising a system that capitalized on necessity.

For example, due to the scarcity of capital, they focused on developing flexible, right-sized machinery and implementing quick changeovers. Additionally, legal restrictions on worker layoffs prompted the cultivation of a strong sense of community within the company, laying the groundwork for extensive employee involvement and collaborative problem-solving.

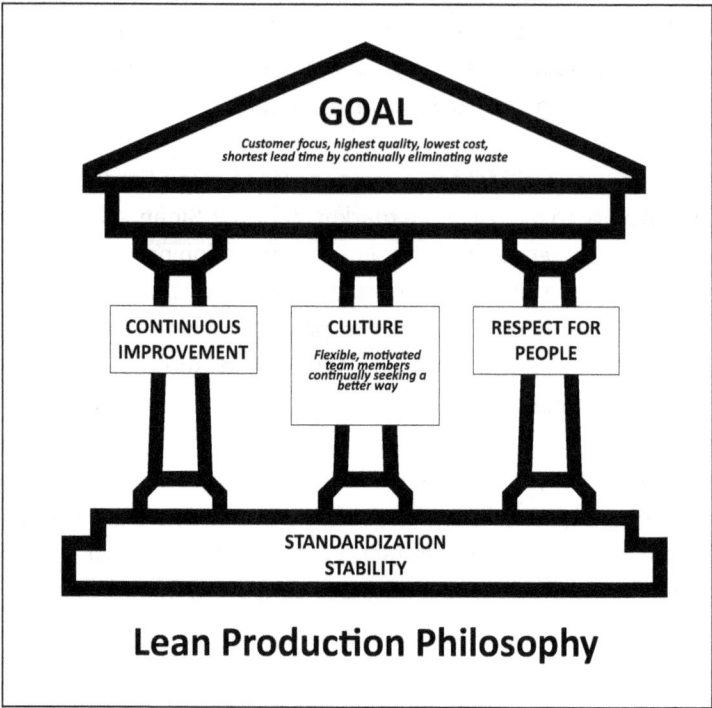

GOAL

Customer focus, highest quality, lowest cost, shortest lead time by continually eliminating waste

CONTINUOUS IMPROVEMENT	CULTURE	RESPECT FOR PEOPLE
	Flexible, motivated team members continually seeking a better way	

STANDARDIZATION STABILITY

Lean Production Philosophy

LEAN PRODUCTION SYSTEM

A key objective of the Lean system is to minimize waste in order to enhance profitability, which is the most effective approach in the context of the new economics. Lean activities are interconnected, mutually supportive, and guided by the same principles.

The eight types of muda ("waste") and the related concepts of mura ("imbalance") and muri ("overburden") are fundamental aspects of Lean practices. Overproduction is considered the most significant form of waste. However, Lean production goes beyond simply seeking out and eliminating waste. It also aims to establish a smooth workflow that allows the customer to pull and to involve our employees in improvement initiatives.

STABILITY

5S and TPM are two crucial elements for achieving production stability. 5S is a process for optimizing and standardizing the workplace to support visual management. Visual management involves managing by exception in a visual gemba. Any out-of-standard conditions are immediately apparent and can be quickly corrected using countermeasures.

The implementation of 5S typically leads to total productive maintenance (TPM), where production team members become involved in basic maintenance activities. TPM focuses on addressing the six significant losses that affect equipment. The Machine Loss Pyramid concept emphasizes the importance of identifying hidden and minor failures. By involving our production team members in checking and improving equipment performance, we can reap substantial benefits.

STANDARDIZED WORK

The goal of standardized work is to identify waste (muda) and continuously improve with the involvement of all team members. Lean production and methods engineering have different approaches to standardized work. Standardized work aims to increase the amount of value-added work in each process, thereby enhancing labor density, and also to improve efficiency by reducing the workforce. The underlying objective of standardized work is Kaizen, the Japanese term referring to improvement activities. Workers who are freed up by Kaizen activities are reassigned.

JUST-IN-TIME PRODUCTION

Just-in-time (JIT) means producing the correct part in the right quantity at the appropriate time. The main goal of JIT is to create a continuous flow of value so that the customer can pull products as needed. JIT also enables quick response to customer demands, a better understanding of takt time, and control over abnormalities. The JIT system consists of Kanban and production leveling, also known as heijunka, along with the six Kanban rules:

1. Never ship defective items
2. The customer withdraws only what is needed
3. Produce only the quantity withdrawn by the customer
4. Level production
5. Use Kanban to fine-tune production
6. Stabilize and strengthen the process

In addition, there are three types of pull systems:

Type A: This is the most common type, and it involves replenishing or filling gaps in finished goods or parts stores when the customer withdraws items.

Type B: This type is used when order frequency is low and customer lead time is long, such as for custom producers. The pacemaker is typically located farther upstream than in Type A systems, and downstream work proceeds sequentially through FIFO (first in, first out).

Type C: This is a combination of Type A and Type B pull systems running in parallel. High-frequency orders go through a Type A system, while low-frequency orders are processed through a Type B system. Type C systems are ideal for manufacturers producing both high and low-frequency items.

Conveyance plays a significant role in the Lean system, with both fixed time and fixed quantity conveyance being possible. Value stream mapping is a tool that helps us understand our current condition and identify opportunities for improvement (Kaizen).

JIDOKA

The concept of Jidoka was created by Sakichi Toyota and further developed by Shigeo Shingo. Jidoka is crucial for achieving the highest quality standards at the lowest cost and in the shortest possible time. It requires a fundamental shift in quality management, moving away from statistical quality control towards 100% inspection and poka-yoke. Poka-yoke is a simple, cost-effective, and reliable tool that inspects all items, detects potential errors that could lead to defects, and provides immediate feedback for taking corrective action. Team members are the best resource for developing poka-yokes.

Poka-yokes either stop equipment or provide warnings when an error is detected. They typically identify abnormalities in product characteristics, variations from a set value, or missing process steps. Sensor technology offers extensive support for poka-yoke development, including both contact and non-contact sensors.

CHAPTER 8

Lean Into Quality With QCD

"Watch costs, and the profits take care of themselves."

— Andrew Carnegie

As a shop manager, it is crucial to prioritize providing customers with exceptional value. To achieve this, one effective approach is to focus on Lean quality, where the QCD processes (quality, cost, and delivery) intersect. Lean quality emphasizes the continuous improvement of processes, reduction of waste, and optimization of resources to enhance the overall value provided to customers.

By incorporating Lean quality principles, shop managers can ensure a more efficient and customer-centric operation, ultimately leading to greater customer satisfaction and loyalty.

Lean quality is a vital component of the Lean production philosophy, which aims to optimize manufacturing processes and minimize waste. This approach evaluates six critical elements: (1.) the quality of the finished products, (2.) ensuring timely delivery of goods, (3.) managing inventory levels, (4.) maximizing equipment efficiency, (5.) adding value at each production stage, and (6.) efficiently utilizing floor space. Businesses can streamline their operations and improve overall efficiency by focusing on these areas.

It is crucial to understand that quality, cost, and delivery are not standalone objectives but rather interconnected. Purchasing products or services without quality is futile, no matter how appealing the price. Similarly, providing products or services with good quality and an attractive price is pointless if they cannot be delivered on time to meet customer needs. This interconnectedness underscores the importance of balancing these objectives.

As a shop manager, you carry the responsibility of finding a delicate balance between quality, cost, and delivery to ensure your business's success. This balance is not just a matter of juggling numbers but a strategic decision that can significantly impact your business's performance. Let's take a closer look at how you can navigate this balancing act.

MORE THAN A RESULT, IT'S A PROCESS!

Quality is not only about the physical characteristics of your products but also includes the processes and services used to produce them. In fact, quality is more than just a result; it's a critical link throughout your company's value chain, involving collaboration between various departments such as sales, design, engineering, purchasing, project management, fabrication, and installation.

Before production starts, the client services team, or upstream management, must set quality standards for planning and deployment. It's vital to grasp customer needs thoroughly, translate them into design and engineering requirements, and make advanced preparations to ensure a seamless start and finish without any interruptions or undesirable effects due to poor planning or communication.

PROCESS EXCELLENCE

Client services and production departments have distinct viewpoints on quality. Client services primarily focuses on business development, project management, and ensuring that the client's needs are met.

On the other hand, the production office is concerned mainly with manufacturing proficiency, including factors that contribute to variability. These factors may include workmanship, equipment efficiency, machine calibration, adherence to standard operating procedures, raw material quality, and production scheduling. The production department's primary goal is to ensure that the manufactured products meet quality standards and customer specifications.

ACT
PROCESS
EXCELLENCE

ACCURATE
COMPLETE
TIMELY

To minimize variations in output, management must set clear standards, foster a sense of self-discipline among employees, and guarantee that no defects are perpetuated. This approach is commonly called "Do not accept defects, do not create defects, and do not pass on defects." A culture that prioritizes adherence to standardization and emphasizes delivering precise, comprehensive, and timely work is the bedrock of quality.

COST MANAGEMENT

It is important to understand that cost management isn't just about cutting costs but also about controlling them. Cost control aims to minimize expenses without compromising on quality. To reduce costs, managers need to carry out various activities in the plant. It is important

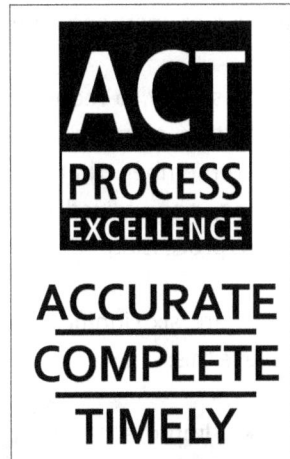

to note that cutting corners, eliminating employees, restructuring, and pressuring suppliers to reduce costs is not the right approach. This tactic can disrupt operations and lead to a decline in quality.

The best way to reduce costs is to eliminate muda, which is a Lean production term for waste. The acronym DOWNTIME can help you remember that muda stands for defects, overproduction, waiting, non-utilized talent, transportation, inventory, motion, and excess processing.

There are six significant cost-reduction activities that can help you achieve this:

- Improve the quality of finished products
- Enhance productivity and ensure timely delivery
- Reduce stock levels to minimize inventory
- Decrease machine downtime to improve equipment efficiency
- Improve shop layout to save space
- Reduce lead time to add value

Implementing these actions will reduce the overall costs of producing your products and services. Let's analyze each of these a little further.

IMPROVE THE QUALITY OF FINISHED PRODUCTS

This can be achieved by enhancing work processes, which results in fewer errors and rejections and reduces the need for rework. It also shortens the lead time and lowers the use of resources, all of which ultimately reduce overall costs.

Process quality refers to developing, manufacturing, and selling products or services in a plant. It specifically refers to how products or services are produced and delivered. Process quality involves managing resources on the shop floor (including worker activity), machinery, materials, methods, and measurements—collectively known as the 5 Ms.

ENHANCE PRODUCTIVITY AND TIMELY DELIVERY

Improving productivity can be achieved by making your current system more efficient without additional input or by adding more resources such as better technology and workers. Keep in mind, the former is more desirable and should be practiced first, because it is less capital intensive and takes less time. For example, having fewer employees can lead to cost savings and fewer quality issues, as fewer hands mean fewer opportunities for errors.

It is important to note that productivity improvements should not result in employee layoffs. Instead, management should view employees freed up by improvement activities as resources for other value-added activities and innovation efforts. When productivity improves, costs go down.

REDUCE STOCK LEVELS TO MINIMIZE INVENTORY

Inventory management can be a major challenge for small and medium-sized businesses. It takes up valuable space, extends production timelines, creates unnecessary movement and storage requirements, and ties up capital. Having too much inventory doesn't provide any additional value; instead, its value diminishes over time and it can quickly become obsolete if the market shifts or competitors introduce new products.

DECREASE MACHINE DOWNTIME TO IMPROVE EFFICIENCY

Equipment breakdowns can lead to production interruptions, additional costs, and reduced quality. Unreliable machinery results in more work in progress, extra inventory, and increased repair efforts, all of which raise operational costs. Also, assigning inadequately trained newly hired employees to machinery can cause delays that are as costly as equipment breakdowns. It is crucial to invest in regular maintenance and employee training to prevent these issues.

IMPROVE SHOP LAYOUT TO SAVE SPACE

A lot of sign companies have non-functional equipment, workbenches, and other unnecessary items taking up space in their shops. To improve production efficiency, businesses can use Lean 5S techniques to organize their production areas, reduce inventory, and minimize transportation and movement requirements. This approach frees up valuable space that can be used to add new production lines or for future expansion.

REDUCE LEAD TIME TO ADD VALUE

The lead time of a company begins when a customer order is accepted and ends when the delivery is signed off. Some accountants suggest it starts when materials are allocated and ends when payment is received.

Regardless of the method used to measure it, reducing lead time is crucial for achieving growth and profitability. Shorter lead times imply better resource utilization, increased flexibility in meeting customer demands, and lower overall costs. A company's efficiency is best measured by its lead time, and management should prioritize shortening this cycle. Reducing lead time waste presents a significant opportunity for ongoing improvement.

ROLE OF THE GEMBA

Gemba is a Japanese word meaning "real place" that has now been adapted to convey "workplace" where value is added. In production, it usually refers to the plant floor.

If a shop's procedures are complex and inefficient, they can lead to defects and machine downtime. This, in turn, can make it harder to meet customer demands for high-quality, low-cost, and prompt delivery and can also make it challenging to reduce inventory levels. Therefore, it's necessary to improve shop operations to achieve QCD improvement.

If the shop is unreliable or not robust enough, improvements in other functional areas—such as design, engineering, purchasing, marketing, and sales—will not be sustained. To achieve continuous improvement, we should start at the shop floor. By identifying and addressing the problems that arise in the shop, we can identify the shortcomings of other supporting departments.

The shop reflects the quality of the company's management systems and helps us see the actual capabilities of management. In other words, progress on the shop floor helps reveal management shortcomings upstream.

DELIVERY

The timely delivery of products and services is crucial to meeting customer demands while maintaining quality and cost targets. Implementing a just-in-time (JIT) system can help reduce costs by synchronizing the supply chain resources. JIT eliminates the expenses of excessive inventory and enhances flexibility within the management system. It can improve quality, pricing, and delivery.

IMPROVING QUALITY REDUCES COSTS

Improving quality and reducing costs are closely linked. Quality forms the basis for efficient cost management and delivery systems. Enhancing both quality and affordability is feasible to satisfy customer needs.

Companies that believe superior quality comes with a higher price are at risk from competitors who provide equivalent or superior quality at a lower cost. Prioritizing quality is crucial for achieving improved, quicker, and more profitable results.

CHAPTER 9

Lean 5S Gets More Work Done Faster

"Good workplaces develop beginning with the Lean 5Ss.
Bad workplaces fall apart, beginning with the 5Ss."

— Hiroyuki Hirano

After being invited to speak at a sign industry forum attended by shop owners and managers, I delivered a presentation on how fabrication shops can enhance their throughput and on-time performance using Lean management principles.

During the Q&A session, an attendee questioned why I hadn't dedicated more time to discussing Lean 5S. I was initially surprised by the query, as I had assumed that 5S was a widely adopted practice. However, it became evident that, while many are familiar with the term "5S," only a handful truly comprehend its essence and even fewer have successfully implemented it.

Following the forum, the group toured a large multinational manufacturing facility, and I was profoundly impressed by their execution of 5S.

The factory floor was impeccably clean and well-organized, and the workforce exhibited remarkable synergy, working cohesively to surpass customer expectations and outperform competitors. Witnessing their successful 5S implementation underscored the potential benefits of Lean production in various industries over the past five decades. It became evident that Lean production is indeed a sensible and proven practice worth contemplating for implementation.

WHAT IS LEAN?

Minimizing waste and inefficiencies is crucial to optimizing the production process. Lean production offers a range of advantages, including reduced waste, heightened productivity, improved quality, increased flexibility, and enhanced customer value.

Under Lean production, eight types of time-consuming "wastes" have been identified, which can be recalled using the acronym DOWNTIME:

Defects: This refers to the effort and resources spent correcting errors and defects in the production process.

Overproduction: This occurs when more products are made than required, leading to unnecessary costs and excess inventory.

Waiting: This is the idle time when processes or tasks are not completed on time, leading to inefficiencies.

Non-Utilized Skills: This waste occurs when employees' skills and talents are not effectively utilized, leading to a lack of employee engagement and suboptimal performance.

Transport: This involves unnecessary movements of materials or products within the production process, leading to additional costs and time wastage.

Inventory: Excess inventory ties up capital and storage space while also increasing the risk of obsolescence and damage.

Motion: Unnecessary movements or actions that do not add value to the production process.

Excess Processing: This refers to any unnecessary steps or processes that do not add value to the final product and should be eliminated to improve efficiency.

WHAT IS 5S?

5S is one of the tools in the Lean methodology toolbox. It is a workplace organization process designed to make work environments more efficient and effective, thereby making work faster. The name 5S is derived from the five stages of this Lean methodology, which originated from Japanese automakers during their post-WWII economic rebuild. Each of the five stages starts with the letter S, hence the term "5S."

The five elements that describe each stage are as follows:

1S - SORT (clear by red tagging)
2S - SET IN ORDER (get organized)
3S - SHINE (clean it)
4S - STANDARDIZE (establish standards)
5S - SUSTAIN (discipline)

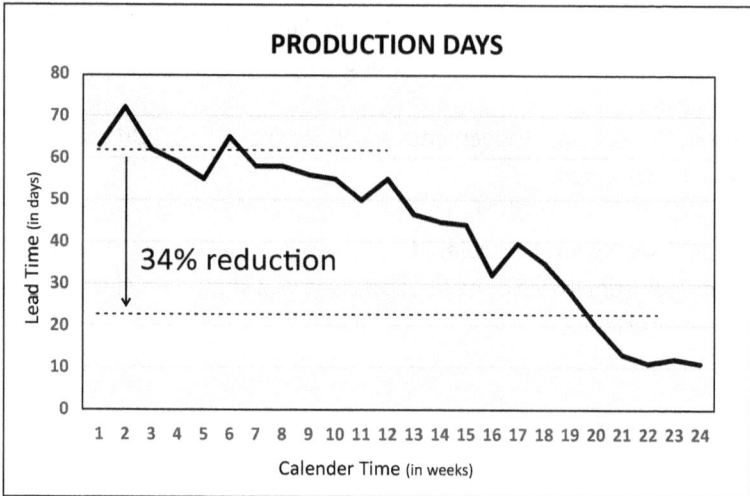

PRODUCTION DAYS

34% reduction

Lead Time (in days)

Calender Time (in weeks)

5S reduces different forms of "waste" that do not bring value to your people or customers.

The visual representation in the graph above demonstrates the significant achievement of one of my clients over a 24-week period by implementing the mentioned strategy. The client realized a remarkable 34% decrease in production turnaround time, reducing the average duration from 59 days to less than 20 days.

It's important to note that these improvements specifically pertained to custom design-build projects, and it was observed that those involved in the production of predefined product lines could potentially achieve even more impressive outcomes.

HOW DOES 5S WORK?

Adhering to the five stages in a specific sequence is crucial to successfully implementing 5S. The process consists of Sorting, Setting in Order, Shining, Standardizing, and Sustaining.

It's important to note that, while the steps are theoretically simple, the execution may not always be easy. Commitment to completing the process is essential, as 5S is an ongoing endeavor that requires continual effort and improvement. By regularly cycling through the stages, organizations can effectively cultivate a culture of sustained improvement.

STAGE 1 - SORT

Many shops are filled with items that are rarely, if ever, used. Workers tend to collect things that are non-value added.

To tackle this issue, begin with a gemba (waste walk) to determine the necessary tools and materials. Choose an area to start and place red tags on every item that is not required for the operation, not in the right place, or not in the right quantities.

Move all these items to a central staging area called the "red tag zone." They can only leave this zone when a person can and will actually use them. This way, items are redistributed to an area or workstation where they are needed. Items not required after a certain amount of time, say 60 days, should be sold, removed, recycled, or disposed.

STAGE 2 - SET IN ORDER

In this stage, you will assign a permanent place for your shop's tools, supplies, and materials. First, remove any remaining items from Stage 1 and place them a short distance away. Then, categorize them based on how often they are used (hourly, weekly, monthly, or yearly). Feel free to create categories that suit your needs. After categorizing, place the most frequently used items closest to where they are consumed or processed and place the less frequently used items further away.

After arranging your items in their designated locations, it's crucial to ensure that they stay there and are returned to their specific places after use. Introducing a Visual Management tool, like a shadow board, can significantly bolster organizational efforts. A shadow board, typically a painted board with each tool clearly labeled and outlined, effectively arranges and manages tools.

The main objective of marking each tool's location on the board is to make it instantaneously noticeable when a tool is missing, thereby reducing the risk of productivity loss. This systematic approach helps mitigate disruption during operations by ensuring that necessary tools are always in their designated spots.

By employing the three-second rule, any passerby should be able to quickly identify if something is out of place, helping to maintain an organized and efficient workspace.

STAGE 3 - SHINE

The third stage in the operational process, known as SHINE (clean), involves an activity in which employees may have varying degrees of responsibility, depending on the nature and scale of the operation. By regularly cleaning their designated machines and workstations, operators are more likely to detect minor abnormalities that may arise during use, effectively preventing them from leading to defects in production. Therefore, the objective of the SHINE stage extends beyond simple cleaning; it aims to cultivate a culture where operators actively respond to deviations from the standard, considered a fundamental practice within Lean thinking and behavior.

STAGE 4 - STANDARDIZE

During the standardization step, you will focus on establishing a consistent approach to executing tasks and procedures. The first goal is to establish guidelines for how work should be carried out in the work center, integrating 5S tasks into the regular process flow.

The second goal concerns prevention: setting clear rules to avoid unnecessary item accumulation, procedure breakdowns, and contamination of machines or materials. You should build infrastructure and establish rules to ensure these two goals are met, such as standard operating procedures (SLSMS) and "one page" work instructions.

STAGE 5 - SUSTAIN

The last stage of the 5S methodology, SUSTAIN, is the most demanding. It focuses on maintaining the changes implemented in the previous stages. This phase is particularly challenging because it involves overcoming established behaviors with new ones.

The ultimate objective of the SUSTAIN stage is to internalize and sustain the practices established in the earlier stages, turning them into habitual behaviors. It's important to recognize that people generally resist change, and breaking entrenched habits can be a formidable task. Therefore, preemptive measures to reinforce and uphold the newly established positive behaviors should be considered.

To facilitate the process, several proactive measures can be implemented. These measures encompass the documentation of routines and standard operating procedures in a clear and accessible manner, the creation of informative newsletters or comprehensive guidebooks to disseminate crucial information, the conduction of thorough team and management audits to assess performance and effectiveness, and the regular scheduling of stand-up meetings to ensure consistent adherence to the introduced modifications by you and your team.

CHALLENGES — TEAM BUY-IN AND SUSTAINABILITY

The 5S process will only be successful if upper management is 100% committed and all employees are completely bought in. Everyone needs to understand why it's important to eliminate time wasters that limit flow and cause problems and how to implement the process.

Companies fail at 5S because they don't understand the goal, which sacrifices sustainability. They find reasons to stop doing all the things outlined in this book. Soon, the benefits are mostly gone; people forget what it all means, and throughput drops, lead times rise, and so does cost. Worse, they start losing skilled people because the culture suffers.

Lean 5S is one of the most powerful management strategies that typically yield the biggest returns on your investment, especially at the onset of a Lean transformation initiative. The benefits you can expect to achieve will be greater on-time performance, less stress, improved employee satisfaction, less firefighting for managers, improved customer experience, and, best of all, more money in the bank!

CHAPTER 10

Benefits of Improving OEE

"The real problem is not whether machines think but whether men do."

— B. F. Skinner

Every year, I attend the International Sign Association's ISA International Sign Expo convention. This annual event is an elaborate showcase featuring hundreds of vendors from across the industry eagerly displaying their latest products and cutting-edge technology.

It is not just a chance to browse but a golden opportunity to network and gain valuable insights into the newest products and trends that can contribute to the growth and success of their businesses. I often bring my clients with me, leveraging the convention as a platform to connect with industry leaders and gain a competitive edge.

However, it's crucial to be mindful of the potential pitfalls of impulsive purchases. The allure of these advanced offerings at industry events can sometimes cloud our judgment, leading to new machinery arriving on the shop floor before the existing machines are even paid off. It's vital to weigh the benefits against the costs and consider the long-term implications of such investments, demonstrating a responsible and prudent approach to business.

I can't express enough how exasperating it is to witness the misattribution of productivity problems to the machines when, in reality, it's a matter of how they are managed and serviced. The perceived bottlenecks are unfounded, akin to fake news. One effective way to address this "buyer syndrome" is by understanding Overall Equipment Effectiveness (OEE) and integrating it into your operations to maximize throughput and profitability.

WHAT IS OEE?

Overall Equipment Effectiveness is a metric utilized to assess the efficiency of manufacturing processes and individual equipment. It is commonly employed in the manufacturing industry to pinpoint areas for improvement, monitor enhancements, and compare the performance of various equipment and production lines.

Before discussing OEE any further, let's briefly consider the current impact of AI and its related technologies, also known as Industry 4.0, the "Fourth Industrial Revolution," or "4IR." This term refers to the rapid technological advancements in the 21st century.

Industry 4.0 can be defined as the integration of intelligent digital technologies into manufacturing and industrial processes. It encompasses a set of technologies that include industrial IoT networks, AI, Big Data, robotics, and automation.

As the signage industry rapidly embraces Industry 4.0 technologies, understanding and integrating these concepts is crucial for your business's long-term success and competitiveness. With the advent of Industry 4.0, IoT devices offer real-time data for evaluating and enhancing OEE. This technological revolution holds immense potential for the future of the signage industry, offering new opportunities and ways to enhance operational efficiency.

Now let's get back to discussing OEE, a key performance indicator that can revolutionize your business and significantly improve equipment efficiency and overall productivity!

Overall Equipment Effectiveness considers three essential factors to assess equipment efficiency or a production process—availability, performance, and quality.

Availability: This factor compares the actual production time with the planned production time to determine the equipment's uptime and overall availability for production.

Performance: Performance measures the equipment's operating speed and efficiency compared to its maximum potential output. It considers equipment idling, minor stops, and speed losses.

Quality: Quality reflects the production rate of "good count" products, indicating the equipment's ability to produce quality output without defects or rework.

The OEE is calculated by multiplying the individual scores of these three factors, resulting in a percentage value that provides a comprehensive assessment of the equipment or process's overall effectiveness.

OEE | Overall Equipment Effectiveness

TOTAL TIME	SIX BIG LOSSES	OEE FACTORS
THEORETICAL PRODUCTION TIME = 24H PER DAY		
PLANNED PRODUCTION TIME — PRODUCTION NOT PLANNED		
ACTUAL PRODUCTION TIME — AVAILABILITY LOSS	MACHINE MALFUNCTION AND UNPLANNED DOWNTIME / CHANGEOVER TIME AND ADJUSTMENTS	**A** AVAILABILITY
NET PRODUCTION TIME — SPEED LOSS	IDLE TIME AND SHORT STOPS / REDUCED PRODUCTION SPEED	**P** PERFORMANCE
WITH LOSSES — QUALITY LOSS	SCRAPPED UNITS / REWORK	**Q** QUALITY
OEE %		
TOTAL — LOSS IN PRODUCTION	**TOTAL LOSS**	OEE=AxPxQ

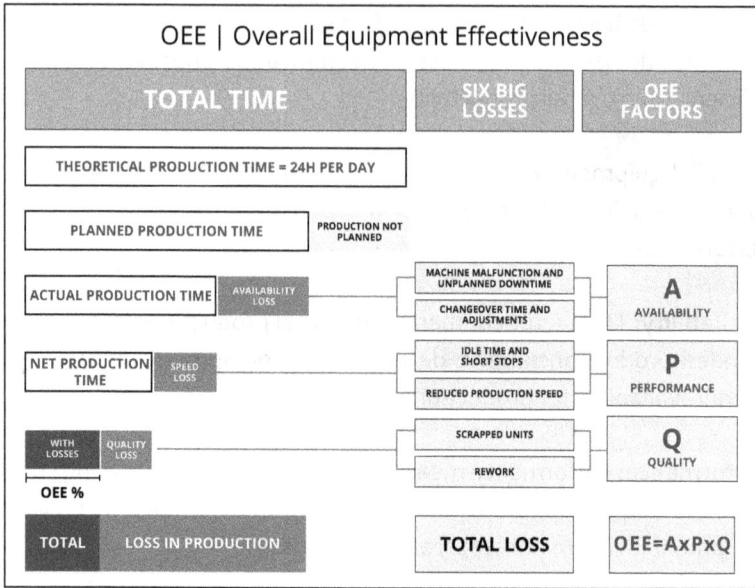

BENEFITS OF IMPROVING OEE

Improving OEE (Overall Equipment Effectiveness) offers several benefits for sign manufacturing organizations, including:

- Increased productivity
- Improved efficiency
- Cost reduction
- Enhanced quality
- Better decision-making
- Increased capacity
- Equipment reliability and longevity

Sign shops can achieve higher production rates, improve overall efficiency, reduce costs, and produce exceptional products that meet or exceed customer expectations by optimizing equipment utilization, reducing downtime, and minimizing quality issues.

Monitoring and analyzing OEE metrics provides valuable insights into equipment performance and production processes, enabling data-driven decision-making and increasing the production system's overall capacity.

Finally, improving OEE often involves proactive maintenance and care for equipment, which can improve equipment reliability, extend equipment lifespan, and reduce the risk of unexpected breakdowns.

HOW TO IMPROVE OEE

Improving Overall Equipment Effectiveness requires a systematic approach. The following are key strategies and practices to help maintain world-class OEE:

1. **Measure and track OEE:** Start by measuring and tracking OEE accurately for your equipment and production processes. Establish a current condition baseline and set goals for improvement. Use OEE as a performance metric to monitor progress and identify areas that need attention.

2. **Focus on availability:** Address equipment downtime and maximize equipment availability. Implement preventive maintenance programs to minimize breakdowns and schedule maintenance activities during planned stops. Optimize changeover processes to reduce setup time and improve equipment utilization.

3. **Enhance performance:** Look for opportunities to optimize equipment performance. Identify and address factors such as availability losses, speed losses, and idle time that impact overall performance. Implement training programs to ensure your operators have the necessary skills to operate equipment efficiently.

4. **Improve quality:** Quality losses can significantly impact OEE. Focus on reducing defects, rework, and scrap. Implement quality control measures, conduct root cause analysis for defects, adopt computer vision technologies to detect anomalies, and ensure quality in manufacturing and production processes. Implement corrective actions to improve product quality and reduce waste.

5. **Implement autonomous maintenance:** Empower operators to take ownership of the equipment through autonomous maintenance practices. Remotely monitor assets from IoT sensors and devices and deploy computer vision at the edge, reducing reliance on maintenance teams and minimizing downtime.

6. **Conduct OEE-driven maintenance:** Use OEE data to prioritize maintenance activities. Focus on critical equipment or components that significantly impact OEE. Implement predictive maintenance strategies by leveraging condition monitoring techniques and real-time data to detect potential equipment failures.

7. **Embrace continuous improvement culture:** Foster a culture of continuous improvement throughout the organization. Implement structured improvement initiatives such as Kaizen events, Six Sigma projects, or Lean manufacturing methodologies to drive ongoing improvement efforts.

8. **Make decisions using data:** Utilize data analytics to gain insights into the factors affecting OEE. Analyze OEE trends, identify patterns, and use this data to make informed decisions about equipment upgrades, process optimizations, or resource allocation. Leverage advanced analytics and predictive models to identify potential areas for improvement.

9. **Engage and train employees:** Teaching and interacting with employees at all levels will drive OEE improvements. Ensure that they understand the importance of OEE, provide them with the necessary training and resources to perform their roles effectively, and involve them in meaningful initiatives. Encourage collaboration and knowledge sharing among teams.

10. **Utilize continuous monitoring and review:** OEE improvement is an ongoing process. Continuously monitor OEE, track performance, and review progress against targets. Regularly assess the effectiveness of implemented improvements and make adjustments as needed. Stay proactive in identifying new improvement opportunities.

Remember that improving the OEE score is a long-term endeavor that requires commitment, collaboration, and a relentless focus on continuous improvement. To maintain motivation and engagement, it's essential to involve all stakeholders (from operators to managers) and celebrate wins.

CHALLENGES FOR IMPROVING OEE

Improving OEE can bring numerous benefits, but organizations may encounter several common challenges when implementing and optimizing it. Below are some of the common challenges organizations face when working on OEE optimization:

Organizational alignment and culture: OEE improvements need a culture of continuous improvement, employee engagement, and effective communication. Resistance to change, lack of buy-in, and a focus on short-term productivity over long-term efficiency can hinder OEE initiatives.

Equipment complexity and variability: Managing OEE for modern production equipment can be challenging due to its complexity and variability. Developing standardized OEE metrics to account for different equipment configurations can be complex.

Understanding OEE metrics: Understanding OEE metrics can be challenging for organizations. Proper training and education can help identify underlying causes of low OEE and prioritize improvement efforts.

Identifying and addressing root causes: Finding the root causes of low OEE is challenging. It requires a systematic approach, data analysis, and stakeholder collaboration—including operators, maintenance personnel, and process engineers. Accurately identifying the underlying issues is crucial for implementing practical corrective actions.

Data availability and accessibility: Real-time production data can be challenging to assess and integrate from different systems and sources, including legacy equipment that may require additional connectivity and sensors.

Sustaining OEE improvements: Maintaining initial improvements in OEE can be challenging. Ongoing measurement and analysis are necessary to maintain these improvements.

Data collection and accuracy: Reliable data collection is essential for accurate OEE calculation. However, manual data entry and inadequate tracking systems can lead to inaccuracies and incomplete information, affecting the reliability of OEE measurements.

Balancing trade-offs: Balancing OEE (availability, performance, and quality) is crucial as improving one aspect may lead to other exchanges, affecting the overall impact on customer satisfaction.

Organizations can effectively implement OEE by proactively identifying and resolving challenges. This approach leads to consistent improvements in equipment efficiency and overall productivity. Though it may seem overwhelming, understanding OEE principles and adopting the related language can help teams make significant progress toward making operational efficiency a competitive advantage.

CHAPTER 11

Concepts of Kaizen

"Progress is impossible without change, and those who cannot change their minds cannot change anything."

— George Bernard Shaw

The term "Kaizen" originates from the Japanese language, and it signifies the principle of continuous improvement. This concept highlights the inclusive nature of improvement, involving managers and workers while emphasizing the requirement for minimal expenditures. The overarching philosophy of Kaizen assumes that every facet of our lives—encompassing work dynamics, social interactions, and domestic life—should be underpinned by a commitment to ongoing improvement efforts.

The Kaizen process involves minor, incremental improvements that lead to dramatic results over time. This concept explains why companies in Japan cannot remain static for long.

In contrast, Western management focuses on innovation, which brings about significant changes in response to technological breakthroughs or new management concepts. Innovation is often dramatic and attention-grabbing, but its results can be problematic because old behavior is so ingrained in the culture, they eventually inch their way back into the system, and management is not willing to commit to the baseline changes. They are on to new shiny things.

On the other hand, Kaizen is subtle and undramatic, focusing on common-sense and low-cost approaches to ensure incremental progress that pays off in the long run. Additionally, Kaizen is a low-risk approach, allowing managers to revert to the old way without incurring significant costs.

KEY KAIZEN CONCEPTS

- Management needs to implement basic concepts and systems to achieve Kaizen's strategy.
- Kaizen and management
- Process versus result
- Following the plan-do-check-act (PDCA) cycles
- Putting quality first
- Speak with the data
- The next process is the customer

Top management plays a crucial and integral role in introducing Kaizen successfully. They need to carefully articulate a clear policy statement, create a detailed implementation schedule, and demonstrate leadership by actively engaging in the Kaizen procedure within their own teams. This active involvement is key to fostering a culture of continuous improvement throughout the organization, making it the driving force behind the process.

Kaizen and management. In the context of Kaizen, management serves two primary functions: maintenance and improvement.

Maintenance encompasses activities that preserve current technological, managerial, and operational standards. This involves upholding these standards through training and discipline to ensure everyone follows standard operating procedures. Under the maintenance function, management performs assigned tasks to sustain the existing standards.

On the other hand, improvement consists of activities geared towards raising and advancing current standards. It involves seeking ways to enhance and evolve the existing processes and procedures. In the Japanese management view, the central principle can be summarized as the dual mandate to maintain existing standards while striving to improve them.

Improvement can be classified as either Kaizen or innovation. Kaizen signifies small improvements due to ongoing efforts, while innovation involves a drastic improvement due to a significant investment in new technology and equipment. Whenever money is a crucial factor, innovation is expensive. Because they are fascinated with innovation, Western managers tend to be impatient and overlook the long-term benefits that Kaizen can bring to a company. On the other hand, Kaizen emphasizes human efforts, morale, communication, training, teamwork involvement, and self-discipline. It is a common sense, low-cost approach to improvement.

Process versus result. Kaizen centers around continuous improvement through a process-oriented approach. It emphasizes that processes must be constantly evaluated and enhanced to achieve better results. When organizations fail to reach their intended goals, it indicates a flaw in the underlying processes, and thus, management must actively identify and rectify these process-based errors. This contrasts sharply with the Western approach, which primarily focuses on achieving results without putting as much emphasis on the processes involved.

When implementing Kaizen strategies such as the plan-do-check-act (PDCA) cycle, standardize-do-check-act (SDCA) cycle, quality, cost, and delivery (QCD), total quality management (TQM), just-in-time (JIT), and total productive maintenance (TPM), it is essential to apply a process-oriented approach. Neglecting this aspect has been the downfall of many companies attempting to adopt Kaizen strategies.

Moreover, the key to success in implementing Kaizen lies in top management's commitment and consistent involvement. Their dedication is crucial in setting the tone for the rest of the organization and ensuring that the Kaizen process is embraced and effectively executed at all levels.

The PDCA/SDCA cycles. The first step in the Kaizen process involves establishing a plan-do-check-act (PDCA) cycle. This cycle ensures the continuity of Kaizen by pursuing a policy of maintaining and improving standards, and it is one of the most important concepts of the process.

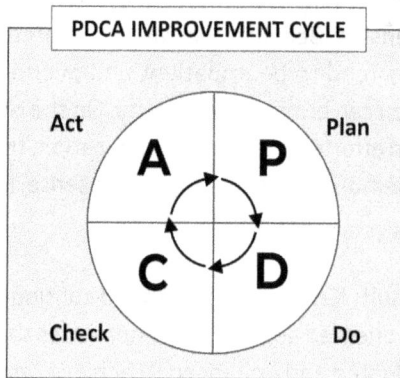

PDCA IMPROVEMENT CYCLE

Act   A   P   Plan

C   D

Check   Do

The PDCA cycle is a continuous improvement process. "Plan" involves setting a target for improvement and developing action plans. "Do" is about implementing the plan. "Check" is about assessing whether the implementation is on track and has led to the planned improvement. Finally, "act" involves standardizing new procedures to prevent the recurrence of the original problem or to set new improvement goals. The cycle then repeats, as the new status quo becomes the target for further improvement. This process is crucial because employees may prefer the status quo and may not always initiate improvements, so management needs to continuously set challenging goals.

Before beginning any new work process, it's important to ensure its stability. This involves implementing the standardize-do-check-act (SDCA) cycle, which helps to standardize and stabilize the current process. This cycle ensures that any abnormality or deviation from the standard is addressed promptly.

When an abnormality occurs, it is crucial to ask the following questions: What is the abnormality? Why did it occur? What should be done about it? And, how can we prevent it from happening again in the future? These questions help to identify the root cause of the abnormality and implement measures to prevent its recurrence. By addressing abnormalities and making necessary improvements, the work process can be stabilized and lead to better outcomes.

Did it happen because we did not have a standard? Did it happen because the standard was not followed, or did it happen because the standard was not adequate? Only after a standard has been established and followed, stabilizing the current process, should one move to the PDCA cycle.

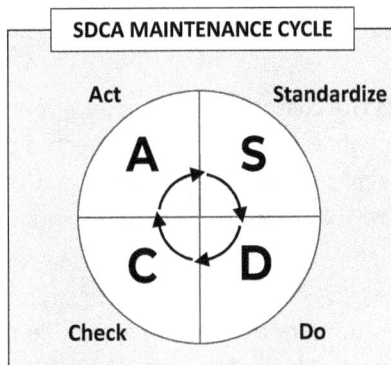

SDCA MAINTENANCE CYCLE

Act — Standardize

A — S
C — D

Check — Do

Thus, the SDCA cycle standardizes and stabilizes the current processes, whereas the PDCA cycle improves them. SDCA refers to maintenance, and PDCA refers to improvement. These become two major responsibilities of management.

Putting quality first. The first step in achieving the primary goals of quality, cost, and delivery (QCD) is to prioritize quality above all else. No matter how attractive the price and delivery terms may be, a company will not be able to compete if its product or service lacks quality.

Embracing a "quality first" philosophy requires commitment from management, as there may be temptations to compromise in meeting delivery requirements or cutting costs. However, giving in to these temptations risks sacrificing not only quality but also the long-term success of the business.

Speak with the data. Kaizen is a problem-solving process. In order for a problem to be correctly understood and solved, the problem must be recognized and relevant data gathered and analyzed. Trying to solve a problem without hard data is akin to resorting to hunches and feelings, which is not a very scientific or objective approach.

Collecting data on the current status helps you understand where you are now. This serves as a starting point for improvement. Collecting, verifying, and analyzing data for improvement is a theme that occurs throughout this book.

The next process is the customer. In any operational workflow, tasks are conducted through a series of interconnected processes. Within this framework, each process is assigned a dual role—it functions as both a supplier to the subsequent process and a customer to the preceding process.

Materials or information are transferred from one process (supplier) to the next (customer), where they undergo further refinement and enhancement. This continual progression ensures that the output from one process serves as the input to the next, facilitating a seamless and efficient operational flow. It's important to note that the concept of the "next process is the customer" extends to both internal (within the company) and external (in the market) stakeholders, ultimately ensuring alignment and collaboration across the entire value chain.

The majority of employees in an organization interact with internal customers. This understanding should lead to a commitment to never pass on defective parts or inaccurate information to those in the next stage of the process. When everyone in the organization follows this principle, the external customers in the market will receive high-quality products or services. As a result, a genuine quality assurance system means that everyone in the organization adheres to and upholds this principle.

MAJOR KAIZEN SYSTEMS

Below are the major systems that should be in place to successfully achieve a Kaizen strategy. Let's take a closer look at each of these:

Total Quality Control/Total Quality Management

One of the principles of Japanese management is total quality control (TQC) which, in its early development, emphasized control of the quality process. This has evolved into a system encompassing all aspects of management and now is internationally referred to as total quality management (TQM).

The TQC/TQM movement provides a clearer understanding of the Japanese approach. Japanese TQC/TQM should not be strictly viewed as a quality control activity. It has been developed as a strategy to assist management in becoming more competitive and profitable by improving all aspects of the business. In TQC/TQM, the "Q" for quality is given priority, but there are also other goals, such as cost and delivery.

The "T" in TQC/TQM stands for "total," meaning that it involves everyone in the organization—from top management and middle managers to supervisors and shop floor workers. It also extends to suppliers, dealers, and wholesalers. The "T" also refers to top management's leadership and performance, which are essential for the successful implementation of TQC/TQM.

The "C" refers to control or process control, and TQM requires the key processes to be identified, controlled, and continuously improved in order to enhance results. Management's role in TQC/TQM is to establish a plan to assess the process in comparison to the results, with the aim of improving the process rather than criticizing it based solely on the result.

TQC/TQM in Japan encompasses activities such as policy deployment, building quality assurance systems, standardization, training and education, cost management, and quality circles.

Just-In-Time (JIT) Production System

This system originated at Toyota Motor Company under the leadership of Taiichi Ohno. Its goal is to eliminate non-value-adding activities and achieve a Lean production system that can handle fluctuations in customer orders. The system is supported by concepts such as takt time, cycle time, one-piece flow, pull production, judoka, autonomation, use of cells, and setup reduction.

To achieve the ideal JIT production system, a series of Kaizen activities must be continually carried out to eliminate non-value-adding work in the gemba. JIT significantly reduces costs, ensures on-time delivery, and greatly enhances company profits.

Total Productive Maintenance

An increasing number of manufacturing companies are now practicing total productive maintenance (TPM) both in and outside of Japan. While TQM focuses on improving overall management performance and quality, TPM emphasizes improving equipment quality. This concept seeks to maximize equipment efficiency through a comprehensive preventive maintenance system throughout the equipment's lifetime.

Like TQM, everyone in the company and everyone at the plant is involved with TPM. The 5S's of housekeeping are another critical activity, and in gemba, they may be seen as a precursor to TPM. However, 5S activities have shown significant achievements in many cases, even when conducted independently from TPM.

Policy Deployment

Although the Kaizen strategy aims to improve, its impact may be limited if everyone is engaged in Kaizen just for the sake of it, without any clear goals. Management should establish clear targets to guide everyone and provide leadership for all kinds of activities to achieve the targets. Implementing the Kaizen strategy at work requires closely supervised implementation, a process called policy deployment or, in Japanese, hoshin kanri.

First, the top management must create a long-term strategy, which should be broken down into medium-term and annual strategies. The top management needs to have a plan to implement the strategy by passing it down through subsequent levels of management until it reaches the shop floor.

As the strategy cascades down to lower levels, the plan should include increasingly specific action plans and activities. For example, a policy statement such as, "We must reduce our costs by 10% to stay competitive" may be translated on the shop floor to increase productivity, reduce inventory and rejects, and improve line configurations.

Kaizen is most effective when everyone works together to achieve a specific target. Management should set that target.

The Suggestion System

An essential part of the individual-oriented Kaizen approach, a suggestion system emphasizes the morale-boosting benefits of positive employee participation. Japanese managers view its primary role as sparking employee interest in Kaizen by encouraging them to provide many suggestions, no matter how small.

Japanese employees are often encouraged to discuss their suggestions verbally with supervisors and put them into action right away, even before submitting suggestion forms. They do not expect to reap great economic benefits from each suggestion. Developing Kaizen-minded and self-disciplined employees is the primary goal. This outlook contrasts sharply with that of Western management, which emphasizes the economic benefits and financial incentives of suggestion systems.

Small Group Activities

A Kaizen strategy includes small group activities and informal and voluntary intra-company groups organized to carry out specific tasks in a workshop environment.

The most popular type of small group activity is a quality circle, designed to address not only quality issues but also issues such as cost, safety, and productivity. Quality circles may be regarded as group-oriented Kaizen activities.

Quality circles have played an essential part in improving product quality and productivity in Japan. However, their role often has been blown out of proportion by overseas observers, who believe that these small groups are the mainstay of quality activities in Japan.

Management plays a leading role in realizing quality in ways that include building quality assurance systems, providing employee training, establishing and deploying policies, and building cross-functional systems for QCDs. Successful quality circle activities indicate that management plays an invisible but vital role in supporting such activities.

The Ultimate Goal of Kaizen Strategies

Since Kaizen is focused on improvement, it's important to identify the areas of business activities that need the most improvement. Quality, cost, and delivery are the key factors to consider.

Quality refers to the quality of both finished products and services, as well as the quality of the processes involved in creating those products or services. Cost refers to the overall cost of designing, producing, selling, and servicing the product or service. Delivery refers to the ability to deliver the requested volume on time. When these three conditions, often referred to as QCD, are met, customers are satisfied.

QCD activities require collaboration across different functions and departments, such as research and development, engineering, production, sales, and after-sales service. Cross-functional collaborations are essential, including those with suppliers and dealers.

It is essential for top management to assess the company's QCD position in the marketplace and establish priorities for the QCD improvement policy.

CHAPTER 12

Lean Shop Management System

"Balance flow, not capacity."

— Eliyahu M. Goldratt

While everything you have read so far is essential for your business's overall success, it all boils down to a simple truth: If you cannot consistently create top-quality products, deliver them on time, and generate a profit, what's the purpose of being in business?

I have had the opportunity to observe, explore, and implement various productivity solutions, ranging from the most expensive ERP software technologies to fundamental whiteboard scheduling methods. These experiences have contributed to creating the Lean Shop Management System™ (LSMS), a practical and applicable system that integrates the best practices and insights gathered over the years.

SIX KEY PRODUCTION SYSTEMS

The Lean Shop Management System™ (LSMS) is a comprehensive production management and quality control process. It is a structured

Production Value Chain consisting of six distinct stages, each meticulously designed to optimize the production process and ensure consistent, reliable results.

The six key production management systems are:

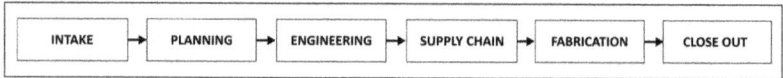

INTAKE → PLANNING → ENGINEERING → SUPPLY CHAIN → FABRICATION → CLOSE OUT

Now, let's examine each stage more closely to help you understand what roles they play.

Stage 1—Intake serves as the primary sub-system within the production management and control system. Its essential role is to act as a "gatekeeper" that plays a crucial part in preventing subpar performance during the subsequent production phases of a project. The core functions of this stage include the receiving of production orders and requests, as well as the critical review process that ultimately leads to the acceptance or rejection of these orders and requests. Despite the seemingly straightforward nature of its functions, the role of Stage 1—Intake is profoundly significant, as it functions as the primary waste preventer in the entire production process.

Stage 2—Planning begins with assessing how work orders or travelers will be organized. This requires a strategic decision-making process to determine whether the configuration will follow a "Batch," "Bundle," or "Single Piece Flow" approach. Carefully considering commonalities between different tasks, along with quantity assessments, forms the foundation for effectively managing line balance and production flow. Additionally, resource allocation and schedule forecasting are integral components of the planning process, ensuring that the necessary resources are available and that production timelines are accurately projected.

Stage 3—Engineering starts with production flow mapping, as discussed in the previous chapter. This approach involves breaking down the manufacturing process into individual steps to identify any potential inefficiencies and to streamline the workflow for optimal efficiency. Engineering and design also involve creating detailed shop drawings and fabrication plans, specifying attachments and construction methodologies, and programming machine runs to determine takt times and materials required for just-in-time (JIT) inventory management. Additionally, routing sequences and release timing for work in progress are carefully considered to ensure smooth operations.

Stage 4—JIT Supply is a key component of the overall just-in-time supply chain strategy, aimed at reducing expenses related to the procurement of subassemblies, materials, and inventory needed for manufacturing specific customer-required products. This involves closely monitoring and managing inventory levels to proactively prevent shortages that could disrupt the manufacturing process. This approach effectively reduces the risk of unused inventory sitting in storage for prolonged periods, thereby minimizing the likelihood of materials becoming obsolete.

Stage 5—Manufacturing involves a wide range of production activities. These activities utilize people, tools, machines, and methods to ensure the smooth flow and coordination of tasks across different work centers. At this stage, production flow and quality are constantly monitored and adjusted, while costs are controlled and evaluated.

Stage 6—Close Out involves analyzing completed jobs and providing team members with detailed reports on various data, such as direct job costs compared to budgets, product performance, production rates, and operational efficiency. This detailed information empowers managers to make informed and strategic business decisions that can positively impact the organization's overall performance and success.

Before delving into the upcoming chapters, it is essential to emphasize the various additional elements that come under the shop management team's responsibility.

PRODUCTION MANAGEMENT TEAM

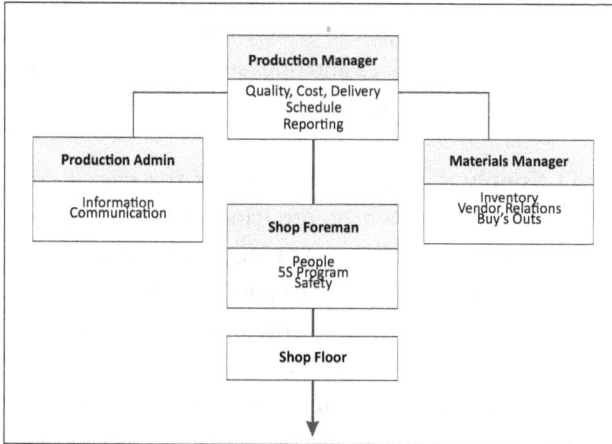

The production management team assumes a pivotal role within the manufacturing process, overseeing tasks from the initial order intake to the final closeout phase. Their primary objective is to supervise shop operations, ensuring a safe and productive work environment for all employees. In larger shops, a full complement of production managers, supervisors, and administrators is typically in place to effectively manage operational tasks, as illustrated in the org chart shown. On the other hand, in smaller-scale operations, the same core responsibilities exist, but the team is usually limited to one or two individuals, creating additional challenges in managing processes and protocols. Despite this, implementing even one lesson learned from this book can result in tangible improvements and reduced stress levels.

Some key responsibilities of the production management team include:

- Optimizing production
- Managing resources
- Ensuring quality
- Maintaining a safe environment
- Managing staff
- Reporting
- Writing procedures

TOOLS TO MANAGE FLOW

In production management, it is crucial to supervise and optimize the smooth flow of manufacturing processes while upholding rigorous quality control standards. Amidst the myriad of methods, checklists, and strategies, eight essential tools form the backbone of a production manager's arsenal. These tools are crucial for ensuring operational efficiency, minimizing errors, and maximizing productivity.

Production Control Files (PCF): This is an essential component of the LSMS. It is a comprehensive repository of job-specific project information and documents that are crucial in managing the production process.

Traveler Queue Processing (TPQ): Maximizing flow is accomplished through a specific sequence of "hold and release" activities designed to balance the flow to the rate of the most constrained resource and limit excess work-in-progress (WIP) on the shop floor at any given time. This disciplined routine draws on principles from the Theory of Constraints and Lean/flow manufacturing.

WIP Task Board: The WIP task board is a tool that sets limits to focus only on the work that can be carried out on the shop floor during a shift. Limiting the amount of work in progress makes it easier to identify inefficiencies in a team's workflow. This is beneficial for recognizing bottlenecks in a team's delivery pipeline before they become significant problems.

Process Control Board: This is a visual display, often a large monitor or magnetic whiteboard, used to illustrate the activities being performed by the production management team. It helps to communicate who is responsible for each task and to track progress by comparing actual performance with planned performance.

Daily Job Status Report (JSR): This tool communicates the status of all work in progress, providing an overview of the collective progress, including job priority, percentage of completion, and information on any delayed or on-hold jobs.

Production Calendar: The production calendar, typically set up within the CRM or ERP system, serves as a visual tool to assist stakeholders in communicating with customers by providing a clear overview of both preliminary and confirmed customer promise dates. It is not intended for task scheduling.

Staging Tags: These visual aids are used to identify different jobs, materials, and their corresponding components. Typically, these labels are attached to bins or racks on the shop floor, providing clear information about the items' placement and contents. They are part of the "Three Second Rule", meaning it should only take an observer three seconds to understand the intention of the items.

Kanban Cards: A tool used in inventory storage areas as part of an effective supply chain management system. These cards act as visual signals, indicating when stock levels for specific items fall below a predetermined threshold. When the inventory reaches the low point marked on the card, it prompts personnel to initiate the replenishment process. This system helps streamline operations by ensuring that products are restocked in a timely manner, reducing the risk of shortages and improving overall efficiency in inventory management.

Task Tickets: These important communication tools confirm the completion of WIP tasks and also track the use of time, materials, and inventory for each job. They provide valuable insights into overall workflow and resource allocation. Although task tickets are sometimes called "time cards," this term is often confused with payroll.

Andon Cards: These cards signal issues that require attention to ensure that projects stay on schedule. When a worker on the production line identifies a problem, such as a defect, malfunction, or safety concern, they notify their supervisors or support teams. In Lean terminology, these reports are similar to the "Andon Cord"—meaning that if there is a problem, production stops, and the issue is resolved before it can harm the overall success of the project. Additionally, these cards serve as the primary data sources for tracking ongoing improvements and Kaizen initiatives.

Job Cost Report (JCR): This report details labor and material expenses for completed jobs, comparing actual costs with the initial project estimate. Job cost analysis helps businesses monitor and analyze expenses for specific jobs or projects.

By implementing a comprehensive system encompassing all key processes, you can gain a highly sought-after attribute that is often challenging for many business professionals to achieve—control!

FREQUENTLY ASKED QUESTIONS

Now that you have read *Lean Shop Makeover*, gained an overview of the Lean production philosophy, and developed some understanding of its history, benefits, team building, and significance to your workforce, you may be curious about why this matters for your business and wondering how to get started. First, let's address some frequently asked questions. While some of these may seem repetitive since I have already covered certain aspects, they reflect the specific inquiries made by prospects and clients.

What is Lean?

Typically, "Lean" refers to the principles of Lean manufacturing, which include.

- Defining value for the customer
- Determining the value stream for each product
- Creating a free flow of materials and raw materials
- Implementing a pull system in the customer-supplier relationship
- Continuous pursuit of perfection
- Eliminating the maximum level of waste and inefficiency in the production process

The advantages of Lean production include reduced waste, increased productivity, improved quality, enhanced flexibility, and improved customer value.

What are its benefits?

- Increases efficiency by up to 66%
- Reduction of inventory in the course of production up to 80%
- Reduction of production space by up to 61%
- Shortening the time of transition from raw material to finished product by up to 70%
- Significant improvement in quality
- Reduction in the number of complaints
- Increase in the number of ideas for improvement presented by employees
- Improved communication
- Reduction of waste

How long does Lean transformation take?

The time to convert to Lean will vary, even if every company takes an aggressive approach. As a rule of thumb, based on my experience, you should plan on at least 2-3 years to reach a reasonable level of competency. Of course, you won't be a great Lean company by then, and you certainly will not be Toyota, but you should have achieved a level where (1.) you will never go back and (2.) the opportunities going forward will be even clearer than when you started.

What is 5S?

5S is a workplace organization tool. By using visual management mechanisms, it is designed to make work environments more efficient and effective. (i.e., worker-friendly).

Each of the five stages starts with the letter S, hence the term "5S". The five words are Sort, Set, Shine, Standardize, and Sustain.

What is the typical ROI for 5S implementation?

To calculate ROI, the benefit (or return) of an investment is divided by the cost of the investment. The result is expressed as a percentage or a ratio. The return on investment (ROI) formula is as follows:

(Money produced after the process improvement – Money produced prior to process improvement) x 100 / Money invested in the process improvement.

The difference between the money produced after the process improvement versus the money produced prior to process improvement is the "Current Value of Investment," which means the revenue or profit obtained from the investment or improvement.

5S IMPACT CALCULATOR		
Number of Employees	35	A
Hourly Wage	$25	B
Shop Rate (cost)	$150	
Number of Days per Year	250	C
5S Current Condition (1-5)	2	D
5S Target Condition (1-5)	4	E
Minutes Saved Per Person, Per Day	40	F
Annual Labor Cost Reduction of 5S Project	$291,667	A x B x C x (E - D) x (F / 60)
New Potential Capacity Per Year Per Person (Hours)	333.33	[F x (E - D)/60] x C
Potential Annual Top-line Growth of New Capacity	$1,750,000	[S sales/ (C x 8 hours)] X New capacity
Estimated Cost of Project	$89,000	Lean Shop Makeover
ROI: Labor Only (Months to Payback)	3.7	(Project cost / Labor savings) x 12

ROI can also be measured by days or months to pay back as shown in the 5S Impact Calculator example above.

Is Lean still a viable solution to today's business?

In a rapidly changing environment, some have questioned the continued relevance and value of Lean manufacturing. The answer is yes, Lean remains highly relevant. Originating from the Toyota Production System, Lean has evolved to equip companies with the ideal tools to navigate today's challenges.

Currently, managing according to Lean philosophy is one of the most effective methods available. It provides development opportunities for individuals eager to engage in the creative process and pursue perfection.

Do we need to purchase software?

No software is necessary; what you have should suffice initially. Your Lean Shop Manager program offers all the systems and tools required to get you started.

How involved does the owner need to be?

The owners must actively participate in driving cultural and mindset change by engaging employees in continuous improvement initiatives. Lean should not be delegated to lower management as a mere checkbox to satisfy customer requirements. Teams play a crucial role in a Lean organization.

What are the biggest obstacles?

The five major challenges to implementing Lean within small businesses include:

- Insufficient management time to support Lean
- Not understanding the potential benefits of applying Lean
- Underestimating employee attitudes/resistance to change
- Insufficient workforce skills to implement Lean
- Backsliding to the old inefficient ways of working

What percentage increase in productivity can we count on?

From a throughput perspective, you should expect at least a 50% increase by the end of year one and a 200% increase by the end of year two.

WHAT CLIENTS CAN EXPECT FROM US

Proven Methodology: Expert guidance is offered to various manufacturers, job shops, and sign and print companies across the United States and Canada. With a hands-on consultative approach and proven best practices, the goal is to enhance your operational profitability, improve overall quality, and establish a competitive edge.

You will be introduced to Lean production philosophy as well as innovative business development methods and systems that can transform your shop in the shortest time possible.

Custom Blueprint for Success: Change initiatives are not a one-size-fits-all solution. Every company is unique and requires careful attention to what makes you and your team special. John will collaborate with you to evaluate your current situation, identify strengths and limitations, and create a comprehensive plan with strategies to achieve your goals. This plan will serve as a roadmap for the decisions and actions that will guide your business's transformation.

Optimize Bottom-Line Performance: By integrating a comprehensive, systemic approach combined with personalized coaching into your existing business structure, you will uncover new avenues for growth and improvement. This dynamic process will equip you with effective, actionable tools designed to maximize your profitability and drive sustainable success. You'll leave with a clear roadmap to enhance financial outcomes and elevate your business to new heights.

WHAT DO YOU GET WHEN WORKING WITH US?

Industry Knowledge: With 40 years of hands-on experience in the sign and visual communications industry, we have extensive knowledge of core manufacturing processes and the products and services our clients provide to their customers, giving us a well-rounded foundation.

Certified Consulting Professionals: Our team of consultants holds certification from the prestigious Association of Accredited Small Business Consultants, ensuring they meet high professional standards. To provide the best support for our clients, they engage in ongoing training that keeps them well-informed about the latest trends and advancements in technology. This commitment to continuous education enables us to offer effective and innovative solutions tailored to the unique needs of each small business we serve.

Companywide Integration: You will start viewing your business as a single system composed of five major subsystems. This perspective will help you transform into a powerful universal business model that effectively illustrates the interconnected nature of all primary areas in your business, including leadership, finance, marketing, management, and operations.

Business Development Focus: This comprehensive program offers valuable insights into systematic processes that are essential for building and sustaining a profitable, competitive, and thriving business. It covers various aspects of business development. You will gain a thorough understanding of key business concepts and strategies, equipping you with insights and skills comparable to those acquired through years of dedicated MBA study. This foundation will enable you to navigate the complexities of the business world with confidence and expertise.

Relationship Networking: You will join a community of like-minded owners and managers, where you can build connections and seek mutually beneficial opportunities. This process involves establishing new relationships, sharing information, and actively assisting others in growing their businesses. Our clients become part of a network of partnerships that can lead to new business opportunities.

Total Resource Library: You will have access to Lean tools, templates, and visual aids. This will reduce the time spent reinventing the wheel during training and system implementation, as best practices have been developed across various industries over many years.

TRANSFORMATION IS A FOUR-STEP PROCESS

A PROVEN METHOD THAT GETS RESULTS!

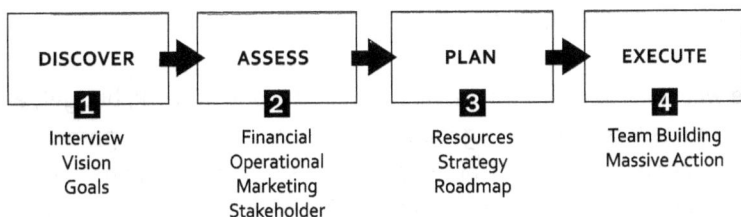

DISCOVER	ASSESS	PLAN	EXECUTE
1	**2**	**3**	**4**
Interview	Financial	Resources	Team Building
Vision	Operational	Strategy	Massive Action
Goals	Marketing	Roadmap	
	Stakeholder		

Step 1: Discovery

We invite you to join us for a complimentary consultation via Zoom, where we will have the opportunity to connect and discuss your specific circumstances in detail. During this engaging session, we will take the time to understand the unique challenges you are facing and work collaboratively to identify potential solutions. This is also a great chance for you to ask any questions or express any concerns you may have. Our team is genuinely excited to assist you and provide the support you need on your journey. We look forward to meeting with you!

Step 2: Assessment

You will receive a comprehensive 10-point operational performance evaluation that thoroughly assesses your business's current health. This evaluation will provide a detailed analysis of various key performance indicators, highlighting areas of strength as well as areas that may require improvement. Additionally, the report will include tailored recommendations designed to enhance operational efficiency, boost productivity, and drive overall business growth.

Step 3: Strategy

We will work together to create a detailed scope of work, budget, and timeline tailored to your organization's specific needs. Our approach will prioritize the most significant opportunities for improvement, ensuring that our collaboration is focused and results-driven. This thorough assessment will allow us to align our plans with your organizational objectives effectively.

Step 4: Implementation

With the plan now established, our team is fully committed to collaborating closely with you and the key stakeholders involved. We will actively engage in the various phases of the project, providing support and expertise to ensure that all tasks are completed efficiently and effectively. Our goal is to facilitate clear communication and a smooth workflow, allowing us to achieve our objectives successfully. Together, we will navigate challenges and make the necessary adjustments to guarantee the project's success.

Celebrate!

Let's celebrate how your organization's culture turns challenges into incredible opportunities for growth! Watch as obstacles transform into meaningful breakthroughs that optimize your processes and create delighted customers. Plus, empowered employees become enthusiastic contributors, energizing a lively workplace and nurturing deeper engagement among all stakeholders. This positive transformation is truly inspiring and drives success for everyone involved!

LEAN SHOP MAKEOVER PROGRAMS

Performance Assessments: This 10-point assessment of operations and production performance is conducted on-site and includes interviews with select management stakeholders, surveys of line workers, general observations of the plant, and a review of key systems, financial metrics, and reporting processes. You will receive an objective, third-party written report detailing the strengths, weaknesses, improvement areas, and recommended solutions.

Lean Shop Makeover: Experience a comprehensive transformation of your production department with our Lean flow management training and the implementation of shop-wide systems. This includes job intake, planning and control, scheduling, employee education and training, job costing, reporting, quality control, supply chain management, and strategies for optimizing shop layout. Our goal is to increase throughput, reduce waste, maintain quality, and minimize stress in your operations.

Kaizen A-la-carte: When a comprehensive makeover is too big a project, you can achieve a small but meaningful improvement without the need for a complete overhaul tailored to your immediate needs.

Oculus Business Development Program: We hold weekly one-on-one Zoom coaching calls designed to provide in-depth instruction on proven practices and theoretical concepts. Each session offers personalized guidance tailored to your specific needs, ensuring a comprehensive understanding of the material. Additionally, participants receive detailed course process guides and customizable system templates to support their learning and application of the strategies discussed during the calls.

In addition to the coaching and educational library you will also become a member of the community forum and mastermind group where collaboration and support is available with other like-minded business owners and managers who are on the same journey.

PUTTING IT ALL TOGETHER

I hope you have found this book insightful and that it has inspired you to take actionable steps toward enhancing your business operations. While the information presented may feel overwhelming at times, I want to assure you that there are numerous paths available to support you on your journey of transformation, no matter where you choose to start.

If you feel that you're not yet ready to make a significant commitment—either in terms of time or financial investment—consider taking smaller, manageable steps. One great way to begin is by furthering your knowledge. I highly recommend reading the companion book, *The Shop Managers Handbook*, which complements the concepts we've discussed here.

Additionally, subscribing to *The Shop Managers Newsletter* will provide you with access to monthly articles, practical tips, and expert advice tailored specifically for shop managers like yourself. These resources are designed to help you gain valuable insights and implement effective strategies in your business.

Moreover, I encourage you to sign up for our educational webinars. These interactive sessions are a fantastic opportunity to learn from industry experts, ask questions, and engage with a community of like-minded professionals who are also focused on improving their businesses.

Our primary objective is to become an integral part of your team and guide you toward success every step of the way. If you are ready to take that first step, please don't hesitate to reach out to me directly. You can also find more information and resources on our website at **www.leanshopmanager.com**. Your journey toward transformation starts today, and we're here to support you.

ABOUT OUR TEAM

John S. Hackley | ASBC is the Founder and Chief Efficiency Officer of Oculus Business Solutions, where he empowers shop owners to achieve remarkable productivity through Lean transformation strategies and effective business management initiatives. With 35 years of proven success in the architectural sign manufacturing industry, he expertly managed over 10,000 diverse projects across the corporate office and healthcare markets. His extensive experience as an accredited small business consultant allows him to provide powerful insights and strategies tailored to his clients' needs. John deeply understands industry trends and continuously enhances his methods by incorporating insights from top business experts. His relentless pursuit of exceptional results positions him as a standout leader in the field.

Jeff Wooten is the Director of Education and Digital Content for Oculus Business Solutions. Jeff boasts over twenty-five years of experience writing about the manufacturing industry. During his long-time tenure as editor of *Sign Builder Illustrated* magazine, he cultivated content that helped a national audience of sign professionals make informed business decisions and learn about how projects were put together. His expertise encompasses a wide range of topics, including signage, digital displays, safety and OSHA regulations, installation, employee management, and marketing. Additionally, Jeff has hosted podcasts and webinars focusing on various subjects of interest related to the signage industry.

To inquire about speaking engagements

please contact John via email or LinkedIn.
Jhackley@oculuscoaching.net

To schedule a free 30-minute discovery call, visit:
www.leanshopmanager.com

Lean **Shop Manager**

Production Management Systems | Shop Makeovers |
Performance Assessments | Business Development | Coaching

Serving the United States and Canada